PSYCHOANALYSIS AND POSITIVITY

PSYCHOANALYSIS AND POSITIVITY

Mariam Alizade

Routledge
Taylor & Francis Group
LONDON AND NEW YORK

First published 2010 by Karnac Books Ltd

Published 2022 by Routledge
2 Park Square, Milton Park, Abingdon, Oxon OX14 4RN
605 Third Avenue, New York, NY 10017

Routledge is an imprint of the Taylor & Francis Group, an informa business

First issued in paperback 2019

British Library Cataloguing in Publication Data

A C.I.P. for this book is available from the British Library

Typeset by Vikatan Publishing Solutions (P) Ltd., Chennai, India

ISBN: 978-1-85575-659-5 (pbk)
ISBN: 978-0-367-32621-0 (hbk)

CONTENTS

A FEW WORDS ABOUT THE ENGLISH VERSION

Positivity was published in Argentina in 2002. My observations on the influence of positivity in my clinical work and the gradual development of this concept at a theoretical and technical level led me to explore new territory. Recent developments in the field of resilience and the psychology of positivity increased my interest in the study of this area.

I am fully aware that there may be resistance to my ideas, not only because of the disturbing newness of this concept in the field of psychoanalysis but also because it appears to contradict or oppose certain principles or ideas regarding the development of the psychoanalytical process.

To my delight and with great interest, I noted that there was a panel at the International Psychoanalytical Congress in 2007 which discussed this theme.

In parallel, I initiated the translation of this book into English with the aim of finding concurrences and points of contentions with colleagues from other latitudes.

It is my wish that to this publication will be added many others from different authors with different lines of thought. I hope that this fusion of ideas will result in theoretical applications and technical modifications which will be beneficial for the cure or psychic alleviation of our patients.

I would like to express my gratitude to the team of translators who worked on this book, and especially to Lesley Speakman and David Alcorn for their helpful comments and revision of the translation.

Buenos Aires
May 2008

INTRODUCTORY REMARKS

This book attempts to explore certain asymptomatic areas of the mind and to integrate them within the overall domain of psychopathological dynamics. It is in these areas that desire, de-alienation and inner freedom play a predominant role. Far from being trivial, the integrative work done on these issues has repercussions on other psychic functions through associative channels. Facilitating pathways are created that open up new avenues; the Oedipal tragedy and the other tragedies that are part of life are made easier to negotiate. In the midst of the clamour of neurosis, *working on health* collaborates in the treatment.

The comedy of life rises to the surface; 'comedy' in this sense refers to representations of different scenarios that present drama, license, naughtiness, and amusement. The multiplicity of these scenarios gives rise to the notion of relativity and minimizes pathogenic events.

Normalcy as a clinical-cum-theoretical concept inevitably features in this book. The positivity of the connection makes itself felt through transference and counter-transference communication.

Without falling into unwarranted enthusiasm or naive optimism, this book examines how positivity operates, and goes on to investigate the concept of the construction of an internal framework, the reversal of repetition, and the problematic issues raised by impasse and trauma.

Just as 'psychoanalytic treatment without tears does not exist'[1] this book argues that neither does psychoanalytic treatment without joyfulness. Tears and laughter are part of the universe of the analyst's consulting room—and in the clinical fluctuation between distress and satisfaction, pleasure and unpleasure, the analyst accepts both extremes. Humour becomes therapeutic as do outbreaks of joyfulness in sessions when the mind is fleetingly freed from the burden of illness.

As a counterpoint to psychic density, there is fragmentation in the ephemeral spaces of pleasurable instants.

Often, as psychoanalytic treatment draws to a close, the work that is accomplished has to do with *consolidating the positive dimension*.

Many conjectures and hypotheses are raised throughout the text; as analysts, we have to follow the different psychic paths as they emerge.

In my conclusion, I discuss the relevance of feelings of joy and happiness.

---

[1] Phrase quoted by E, Pichon Rivière and attributed to Rickmann in Pichon-Rivière, E. (1970) *El proceso grupal. Del Psicoanálisis a la Psicología social.*

CHAPTER ONE

Positivity in psychoanalysis

> The game of science is, in principle, without end. He who decides one day that scientific statements do not call for any further test, and that they can be regarded as finally verified, retires from the game.
>
> Karl Popper (1934, p. 153)

Introduction

I would like to introduce the term 'positivity' into psychoanalysis, with the intention of giving this dimension the status of a concept and of demonstrating how it influences clinical practice and the theory of psychoanalytic technique. Future research will serve to validate or invalidate, partly or completely, my hypotheses. In so doing, nevertheless, new problem situations will emerge that might further our knowledge.

The concept of positivity or the positive dimension arises from a theoretical procedure based on empirical experience. Observation of the effects produced by interpretative and interrogative digression outside the realm of the symptom is crucial to establishing its underlying psychic and structural conditions. I have often come across the situation in which there was a latent positivity in action that was frequently being diminished in strength by layers of psychic pathogens. I had the impression that different pathways and unexplored psychic openings could emerge if more clinical work was done on the positive dimension. After constructing my initial hypotheses, I reworked them as the analytical process and its attendant resistances continued. The empirical confirmation of my hypotheses was gradually strengthened, finding support in certain Freudian conceptualizations, so that my confidence in bringing these ideas to light grew.

The critical rationalism demonstrated by K. Popper (1958) goes beyond the limitations of the narcissistic wound and confronts every research worker with the veracity or otherwise of his or her hypotheses. There is a direct interest in criticizing and exploring possible errors in attendant propositions. The motive force behind this is less the triumph of founding an exact theory than the passion for scientific progress. Thales, in days gone by, encouraged his disciples to call into question what their teachers were professing. He asserted his own fallibility in a clearly non-dogmatic stance, maintaining that only through critical discussion is it possible to approach truth (Popper, 1958).

The dogmatic use of certainty in any discipline means that all thinking stagnates and leads to gradual impoverishment.

'We must be absolutely modern,' wrote Arthur Rimbaud (1873 [1952, p. 198]) a century ago. If we agree with Freud that a certain kind of truth is conveyed by the voice of the poets and we apply this phrase to psychoanalysis, the need to listen to the unknown arises in all analysts.

Driven by the clinical need for greater efficiency, new trends in psychoanalysis call into question certain conventional clinical strategies.

Interdisciplinary parallels[1] create a cultural field ripe for new paradigms. When they reach psychoanalysis, certain discoveries and

---

[1]I would like to thank Fernando Uribarri for reading this chapter and for his contribution to the concept of positivity in philosophy.
Without using the term 'positive', many philosophers have addressed this topic in relation to vitality, creation and evolution. Spinoza, through his emphasis on the

hypotheses give rise to turning points in the conception and application of that science.

Psychoanalysis is subject to the ravages of time and history. *The timelessness of the unconscious must not be confused with the timelessness of our theories.* Cultural conditioning and the manifest or latent influence of the prevailing culture determine the domain of what can be thought or generated as a new thought at any given point in time (Alizade, M. 1996c, 101–107).

The diversity of the positive dimension

The semantics of positivity is not univocal. The positive dimension encompasses states, experiences, dialectic movements, and psychic circuits, as well as meta-psychological considerations and functions.

In order to have some idea of the sheer diversity of the positive dimension, it is necessary to describe different facets of it as a concept. 'Positivity' includes commonsensical spaces as well as abstract spaces of tentative theorizing.

As a philosophical concept, it does not have the same import as the concept of the negative. Ferrater Mora's (1941) philosophical dictionary, for example, makes no mention of this word.

Abbagnano (1960, p. 937) differentiates three lines of thinking in relation to the positive dimension:

1. It expresses what is recognized as a fact—'the basic meaning of this definition of the term is what governs *de facto* or has effective

---

body and passions; Nietzche, in relation to the drive for knowledge and power and his genealogical method, where the difference lies, according to Deleuze, 'not in criticism but in being the positive element of a creation'; Bergson, with his idea of 'vital impulse', connected to intensity, potentiality and virtuality. Closer to psychoanalysis, the 'philosophers of desire' must rate a mention—G. Deleuze, F. Guattari and J.F. Lyotard, who criticize the Platonic legacy, and especially Lacan, who defined desire in terms of something essentially lacking. These philosophers argue that desire is pure positivity, a source of disruption, destiny, evolution and events. Lastly, a major point of reference is the philosophical and psychoanalytic work of Castoriadis, whose notions of radical imagination and social imaginary are defined as sources of 'positive' creation. Irreducible to prior determinants or to any kind of functionality, this current constitutes the 'positive' foundation for an affirmative conception of the subject.

reality'. Positive fact and positive reality are *ipso facto* objective. He cites Schelling, who distinguishes the negative conditions of knowledge, without which knowledge is impossible, from its positive conditions, which render knowledge effective. He also cites A. Comte (Abbagnano, 1960, p. 937) who states, 'According to its oldest and most common definition, the word "positive" names the real as opposed to the fanciful.'
2. It expresses the affirmative.
3. As related to positivism.

The French Robert dictionary (p. 1,354) contains other semantic connotations of this word, such as:

1. What is certain, authentic, useful, effective, concrete.
2. The constructive. Constructive, positive (as opposed to negative, destructive) spirit.
3. The rational.

Green (1993) offers four definitions of the negative: a) the latent, that which is not seen; b) the rejected; c) the absent, the virtual; and d) nothingness. These semantic terms are opposed to the positive series, which is: a) the manifest; b) the accepted; c) the present, the real; and d) the concrete, comprehensible, thinkable.

The constructive aspect of the positive is indissolubly linked to a flexible and vital interaction on both an intra-subjective level and an inter- and trans-subjective level (Puget, J., in Bianchedi E.T., Bianchedi, M., Braun J. & Pelento, M. [1993]).

In keeping with the psychoanalytic perspective, in my approach to the positive dimension I tend to favour the constructive (unconscious and conscious) aspect linked to the life-drive. *It is not enough to destroy sickness. One must construct health.*

The positive dimension

The positive dimension operates on several levels. It seeks to bring forth the positive potential that underlies disturbed mental functioning. It works in the narrow, barely processed zone that is not subject to sickness, the *locus* in the mind where lightness, a favourable disposition and enjoyment filter through. The healthy psychic island, so to speak.

In studying positivity, we pay attention to the part of the patient that is not ill. This psychic zone may be either manifest or latent. If manifest, the positive dimension allows for a direct observation of the patient's life-promoting mechanisms. If latent, that dimension is inferred as an underlying psychic *locus*, often ignorant of its own existence. It is a life-enhancing potential broken down by illness.

As living human beings, we all have some measure of vitality. The positive dimension has to do with material which, when it comes to the surface of the mind, determines to a large extent the evolution of the analysis.

The study of positivity entails reflecting on a certain ideology of suffering in psychoanalysis, one that is both reasonable and iatrogenic. The ideology of suffering sometimes serves as an epistemological obstacle that perpetuates, in the analytic field, the idea that suffering is only resolved through even more suffering. Though partly true, this idea often produces harmful effects by consolidating sterile circuits in the mind that simply resonate with one another.

In our culture, anything that is sombre and evocative of suffering is considered to be coterminous with importance. Perhaps this is due to the influence of our Judeo-Christian upbringing which, riddled with sacrifices and punishments, facilitates a certain degree of masochism. Simple psychic characteristics such as cheerful and trivial are not, given the meaninglessness of life, among the concerns of psychoanalysis. For a session to be really significant, it must entail some degree of suffering. A good analyst really 'goes at' his patient. Levity in any of its forms is not conceived of as having any therapeutic value.

Psychoanalysts have worked mainly with disturbed associations, intolerable representations, suppressed unpleasant affects, and so on. In its first hundred years of existence, psychoanalysis neglected the systematic and precise study of the effects of psychic work in relation to the positive dimension and its impact on mental pathology. What was important in this initial period was the exploration of pathology.

The pleasure—unpleasure system has been the object of numerous observations, starting with Freud. Grief, pain, sadness and *angst* have been rigorously examined. Happiness, joy, well-being, feeling at peace, inner balance and other such sensations have been thought of as 'extra' affects and experiences that emerge once traumas have been placed in a historical perspective and worked through. Positive affects had little value as objects of study in and of themselves. Psychoanalysis, a serious therapeutic tool, could not waste time on happiness.

The positive dimension requires that the analyst explore realms governed by the life-drive and a form of thinking that puts traumatic events or other such tragic circumstances into perspective. Once its full pathogenic scope is acknowledged, the ideology of suffering attenuates harmful effects.

I have considered the advisability of putting forth strategic technical modifications for the sake of clinical efficiency. These new trends aim to avoid the monotony and persistence of a worn-out, repetitive and painful discourse that is immune to any attempt at working-through.

Positivity belongs to a domain that is consistent with mental health, the healthy part of the personality, psychic normality and the tendency of the psychic apparatus to minimize conflict. The masochism guardian of life (Rosenberg, 1991) is reduced to a minimum.

Meta-psychological considerations

I will outline some meta-psychological alternatives that concern the positive dimension, fully aware, of course, that they require further development.

1) Repressed or suppressed unconscious positivity

Unconscious positivity is repressed or suppressed in terms of representations and affects. When it becomes conscious and explores associative pathways, this dimension can participate in the processes of insight. This positivization, however, does not mean that a therapeutic effect will automatically follow on from it. Making the unconscious conscious does not guarantee an outcome based on true working-through.

2) The true unconscious positive dimension
This positivity resides in the depths of the mind as a reserve for the life-drive. This is an invisible positivity, a psychic substance that spills over into the associative circuits, a hidden positive, created by accepting the fact that something is always 'lacking'. It facilitates the opening up of psychic pathways that generate a favourable disposition and soothe the mind (*Erleichterung*) (Freud, 1905c).

Positivity is reached meta-verbally, and cannot be put into words. As a concept, it includes the idea of what cannot be represented, just like the concept of the navel of the dream. This space is related to the unthinkable and to the notion of the unknown outlined by Rosolato, for whom there is definitely something unknown and unknowable. It cannot be abolished and it constitutes the finite as the limit of all knowledge (Rosolato, 1989).

Positivity in the depths of the unconscious facilitates life-promoting impulses.

3) The conscious, deceptive positive dimension (apparent positivity)
Although positive in appearance, this discourse expresses the ego's voluntarism in the service of the death-drive, frequently disguised as libidinal purpose. True positivity is hidden.

4) The conscious positive dimension (manifest, real, concrete)
It is linked to positive action and subsumes the idea of constructiveness. It is the concrete-positive, a fact that constructs in and of itself. This positive form entails unbinding masochist fixations and mental health.

5) The automatic positive dimension
This predominates in 'healthy' minds. Given two pieces of news, one sad and one happy, the happy news is what is focused on and remembered. The sad one is less cathected. This automatic positivity is enacted in all orders of existence.

The memory of traumatic events, whether experienced by the self or by others (events removed from the psyche), is preserved insofar as it is useful or in keeping with a minimal quantum of life-protecting masochism (Rosenberg, 1991). There is no pathogenic masochistic fixation.

6) Positivization of the negative

The no-no is never a 'pure no' and behind many 'yes's' lie destructive impulses.

The positivization of the negative indicates a psychic change of direction that focuses representational and affective circuits on a greater acceptance of constructiveness (understood as the preeminence of the life-drive).

As Ferrater Mora (1941) points out, negation does not directly affect its object. Negation maintains a certain degree of affirmation which affirms, in and of itself, something in the object.

In my work on the dissolution of the Oedipus complex may take on in women (Alizade, 1992 [1999, pp. 127–137]) I presented the idea of positivization in 'not having' as a new category. The positivization of the negative in the dissolution of the Oedipus complex is a crucial stage that allows for a new psychosomatic act. The sign is reversed and equations geared towards positivity emerge. Structural operations highlight the positive aspects of the 'negative' (Alizade 1992/1999). These complex processes are crystallised in a new psychosomatic event.

As I wrote (Alizade 2002, p. 33), 'making the "negative" positive is a psychic mechanism that I have described in earlier papers on femininity and culture (Alizade 1992, pp. 214–215)'. There, I hyposethized the existence of a movement that gradually shifts from negation to affirmation. This form of negation does not affect the object considered. It entails the decline of a 'negative' dimension without excluding the set of positive aspects that may also characterize it. For example, as regards femininity, 'not having a penis' says nothing about what a woman *does* have. Affirming the feminine dimension per se and highlighting its positive aspects relate to equations involving a different *quality* of possessing, and the mental space in which this positive feedback occurs neutralizes the cultural connotations that tend to downgrade women.

D. Anzieu (1990b, p. 55) comments on a type of patient characterized 'by inadequate experience in the realm of transition, negative experience, carried out backwards: it is necessary to detect the sectors for which this experience was erroneous in order to re-establish it positively throughout the psychoanalytic experience'. Rendering the negative positive becomes one of the keys of clinical practice. It requires a kind of reversal of the sign (from negative to positive), a psychic act that will be formulated in terms of repetition.

The reversal of the sign indicates a sort of mental metamorphosis geared towards the construction of de-pathologized functioning.

7) The positive dimension and the drives

Freud writes,[2] 'Affirmation [...] belongs to Eros; negation—the successor to expulsion—to the instinct of destruction' (Freud 1925h, p. 239). The 'yes' to life expressed in a vital stance in the face of obstacles indicates positivity. This conscious or unconscious *erotic affirmation* is laden with psychic consequences. In its reparative work, analysis reinforces the dominion of affirmation and thus unlocks the power of the life-drive that underlies conflicts and pathogenic structures.

This affective, experiential 'yes', is conveyed in the desire for intersubjective exchanges. An individual's degree of positivity interacts experientially with that of others. It is structured in relation to its like, through a deep and mutual influence.

Positivity and affirmation become synonyms and find a metapsychological space that requires close observation. Positive affirmation is at one with the life-drive. It can become a deceptive conscious positive affirmation in which a manifest 'yes' hides evil influences. It is not the appearance but rather the predominant instinctual drive that distinguishes affirmation from negation. A manifest 'no' can be at the service of the life-drive and constitute an ethical 'no', a 'no' that brings order.

When Freud speaks of the importance of an adequate 'taming of the drives' (Freud 1937c, p. 225)—without providing explicit clinical parameters on how to do so—he is referring to a fundamental obstacle to analytical treatment. The drive that must be tamed is always the destructive drive, variously combined with the other drives (the life-drive, the instinct for mastery, the sexual-drive, and so on). The death-drive and its manifestations are what have to be tamed.

[2]The original phrase reads: *Die Bejahung—als Ersatz der Vereinigung—gehört dem Eros an, die Verneinung—Nachfolge der Ausstossung—dem Destruktionstrieb* (1925 *Die Verneinung*, p. 376 TIII *Studienausgabe*).

Healthy psychic functioning makes use of tools that bring to a halt or render inactive destructive impulses.

8) The absolute positive dimension

Just as there is an absolute evil where catastrophe, horror and devastation reside, the idea of an absolute positive dimension gives positivity a rare degree of strength. This *positive power* must be called on to defeat the destructive instinct (Thanatos) on the intersubjective and social level. Here, positivity refers to an absolute good as a cultural imperative. It requires deep psychic transformations that increase the level of psycho-social positivization and allow the death instinct to be sublimated.

CHAPTER TWO

Theoretical fundamentals

This approach to psychoanalytical treatment, with its focus on the dimension of positivity, is based on the following Freudian concepts: 1) facilitation; 2) ramification; 3) infiltration; 4) associative reflection; and 5) the role of the superego.

The concept of facilitation

In his *Project for a Scientific Psychology* (Freud, 1950 [1985]) Freud introduced a new orientation, his intention being 'to furnish a psychology that shall be a natural science' (p. 295). In this text, psychology and neurophysiology merge in a unique attempt to understand the intimate relationship between psychical processes and their biological basis.

Freud distinguished between impermeable 'Psi' Ψ neurons, and permeable 'Phi' Φ neurons. Ψ neurons have 'contact-barriers' whose state is a measure of the 'degree of facilitation' (*Bahnung*) that is present in the system (p. 300). The change in the state of facilitation of Ψ neurons after an excitation constitutes memory.

The concept of facilitation is linked to that of conduction and of 're-learning' (p. 300), all of which relate to the representation of memory. When contact-barriers between neurons are more capable of conduction and less permeable, the degree of facilitation is increased. 'The memory of an experience (that is, its continuing operative power) depends on a factor which is called the magnitude of the impression and on the frequency with which the same impression is repeated' (p. 300). This effect, when positively oriented, has a primary role in the patient's cure.

Facilitations become agents of discharge whose function is to prevent the overburdening of the psyche by releasing large amounts of quantity (memory), thus relieving the psychical apparatus and protecting it by means of these neuronal screens.

In Freud's conception of this neuronal network, each neuron has several pathways which interconnect with other neurons. The choice of the pathway is directly related to the function of facilitation. After many reformulations of his hypothesis, Freud concludes that there are 'permanent facilitations' (p. 302) which may only be a remnant of the initial facilitation which took place after a passage of quantity. The neuron has learned to respond to a lesser stimulus with the same reaction. What exists, therefore, is *neuronal learning*.

With respect to the experience of satisfaction, Freud wrote: 'Once again, cathexis is here shown to be equivalent, as regards the passage of *Qn* [quantity], to facilitation' (p. 319).

Facilitation leads to a certain degree of psychical automatization in that associations of thought and affect learn to use certain paths which are revisited time and time again. Certain ways of thinking become a type of reflex action. These facilitated pathways are closely related to substitute formations wherein a false pathogenic connection repeatedly produces harmful effects on the psyche.

Facilitation depends upon quantity and upon the number of times in which this process is repeated. Repetition is, therefore, a prerequisite to bringing about change, this being the reason why psychoanalytic treatment, in many cases, requires a high frequency of sessions.

Freud noted the repeated failure of the psyche's primary trend to avoid pain. He states that pain was 'the most imperative of all processes' (p. 307) and concludes that it 'no doubt leaves permanent facilitations in Ψ—as though there had been a stroke of lightning' (p. 307).

The study of the dynamics of facilitation leads us to infer that *new facilitations* or the psychic imprinting of new experiences can be therapeutically established so that they may break, interrupt or lessen the cathexis of pathogenic ones. It may be the case that the analyst can use their key position in the analytic dyad, which allows them to steer the course of the treatment, so that by simply ignoring these negative facilitations, they can be neutralized.

This focus on what is positive cathects the patient's pleasant representations, retrieves happy memories and challenges permanent, painful facilitations. How then can new, positive facilitations be created?

The constant recounting of traumatic or harmful memories, if not accompanied by the process of working-through, may lead to a kind of inoperative facilitation, fixing unpleasant mental associations so that there is little hope of a positive mental outcome. In contrast, opening up new ways of thinking linked to positive, pleasant memories can give rise to, or intensify, what I call *positive facilitations*, which provide the psyche with a source of good mental health able to neutralize pathological aspects of the patient's mind. At the same time, these new psychical paths may challenge both individual and transgenerational destructive mandates. The increase in positive facilitations strengthens the life-drive. When discussing the relation between facilitation, desire, and memory, Valls writes: 'Desire attempts to relive the intensity of the sensation felt with the object at the point when the representation—a remnant of the mnemic trace left by the experience—was formed' (Valls, 2004 p. 64).

This concept of neuronal learning has a bearing on the redundant repetition of memories and experiences, both traumatic and non-traumatic, in different analytical sessions. In cases in which interpretation repeatedly fails because the material cannot be worked through by the patient, a potential *re-traumatizing overlearning* is likely to occur. We should bear in mind that this kind of analysis is not beneficial, inasmuch as it hinders the progress of the treatment and heightens resistances, which may become chronic.

The specific task of the analyst, as a fellow-being wishing to help their vulnerable patient, is to provide the psyche with experiences of primitive satisfaction. In the analytic dyad, the patient becomes attached to the analyst in order to receive from them a form of psychic sustenance, which facilitates the analytic process.

The encounters between analyst and analysand are continued experiences which provide the mental substrate for repetition, learning, and the gradual acquisition of new facilitations.

When the psyche is detoxified of unpleasant memories the likelihood of a positive outcome is increased. To the classic method of psychoanalysis, I would therefore like to suggest adding another, whose goal is to create and strengthen the patient's positive attitude.

The process of ramification

As previously mentioned, redundancy can produce facilitation. This principle leads us to reflect on those experiences that are remembered or repeated by the patient time and again, especially as regards the chronic *hyper-representation* of painful experiences.

The theory underlying this hyper-representation asserts that it is the only way to resolve and work through a traumatic situation. This is only partially true. The analyst should also act as a protective screen against the traumatic accumulation of pathogenic material.

There are two mechanisms that help protect the psyche:

1. Stimulation of non-pathological facilitations.
   This is bound up with the process of building good mental health.
2. Ramification.

Freud describes this process in Chapter 9 of the *Project for a Scientific Psychology* entitled 'The Functioning of the Apparatus'. He shows that a powerful stimulus passes along multiple paths, and concludes that: 'The sensory path of conduction in phi/Φ is constructed in a peculiar fashion. It ramifies continually and exhibits thicker and thinner paths, which end in numerous terminal points ... Thus, quantity in psiΦ is expressed by *complication* in phiΨ' (pp. 314–315). Ramification protects the psyche by not allowing all cathexis to be focused on the same place.

These protective ramifications alleviate and lighten the psychic burden of suffering. Using this awareness of *the transformation of quantity into complexity*, the analyst endeavours to interweave bearable representations with unbearable ones, thus forcing traumatic linearity to deviate from its destructive course by means of *the process of ramification*. In this way, the process of *retraumatization* is brought to a halt and new positive, psychical pathways are created, based on which the individual may learn a new approach to life.

By using this process of ramification, and by interlinking positive representations and affects with negative ones, the potential effectiveness of treatment may be enhanced.

Infiltration

In considering the disruptive effects of mental illness, Freud distinguishes between a foreign body and an 'infiltrate':

> We have said that this material behaves like a foreign body, and that the treatment, too, works like the removal of a foreign body from the living tissue. We are now in a position to see where this comparison fails. A foreign body does not enter into any relation with the layers of the tissues that surround it, although it modifies them and necessitates a reactive inflammation in them. Our pathogenic psychical group, on the other hand, does not admit of being cleanly extirpated from the ego. Its external strata pass over in every direction into portions of the normal ego: and, indeed, they belong to the latter just as much as to the pathogenic organisation. In analysis, the boundary between the two is fixed purely conventionally, now at one point, now at another, and in some places it cannot be laid down at all. The interior layers of the pathogenic organisation are increasingly alien to the ego, but once more without there being any visible boundary at which the pathogenic material begins. In fact, *the pathogenic organization does not behave like a foreign body, but far more like an infiltrate* [my italics]. In this simile, the resistance must be regarded as what is infiltrating. Nor does the treatment consist in extirpating something—psychotherapy is not able to do this for the present—but in causing the resistance to melt and in thus *enabling the circulation to make its way into a region that has hitherto been cut off* [my italics]' (Freud, 1895d, pp. 290–291).

The infiltration model confirms the relevance of working in areas not yet contaminated by pathology. In the same way that the pathogenic organization invades the psyche, *the non-pathogenic organization may overpower and prevail over mental illness.* A model is established in which one area dominates the other. This line of thinking, based on a dualist conception, emphasizes the value of alleviating pain and suffering by means of abreaction and working-through, while simultaneously working with non-pain—pleasure, well-being—in order to strengthen and expand this psychical area. Analytical treatment not only brings about the 'infiltration' of well-being as a consequence of the resolution of conflicts, but also does so within the framework of *specific positive action*. This action neutralizes the Thanatic power of internal conflicts over mental stability, a key factor in the building of good mental health.

Associative reflections

At the beginning of his career, Freud referred to the psychical mechanisms of healthy individuals when defending themselves from the effects of a psychical trauma:

> Abreaction, however, is not the only method of dealing with the situation that is open to a normal person who has experienced a psychical trauma. A memory of such a trauma, even if it has not been abreacted, *enters the great complex of associations* [my italics], it comes alongside other experiences which may contradict it, and is subjected to rectification by other ideas. After an accident, for instance, the memory of the danger and the (mitigated) repetition of the fright becomes associated with the memory of what happened afterwards—rescue and the consciousness of present safety. Again, a person's memory of a humiliation is corrected by his [*sic*] putting the facts right, by considering his own worth, etc., In this way a normal person is able to bring about the disappearance of the accompanying affect through the process of association (Freud, 1893–1895, p. 9).

The process of association is focused on the traumatic event, but requires the help of 'rectifying' ideas, that is *corrective representations.*

The healthy person's *reflections,* which Freud drew attention to, help an individual to overcome a traumatic incident.

Freud highlights that conscious thoughts can have a curative effect insofar as they enter and become part of the vast field of psychical associations. The terms 'reflections' and 'infiltrations' are closely related in that both clearly demonstrate the complexity of psychical interrelationships.

The role of positivity comes into play when traumatic representations are bound to non-traumatic ones in a delicate balance (interweaving) that restores the psyche to its original state of equilibrium. The notion of *associative reflections* introduces the idea of a psychic process of enormous potential in clinical work.

Some notes on the superego

The stimulation of the health-enhancing functions of the superego is a cornerstone of the working hypothesis related to treatment which focuses on the positive dimension.

Hypothetically, the superego is composed of three parts: the ego ideal, self-observation, and moral concience, each of which has its own facets, contents, functions, intrasystemic relations and dependencies.

The contents of the superego are essentially objects, conflicts, affects, and identifications. Its functions are based on prohibitions, regulations, exhortations deriving from 'its compulsive character, which manifests itself in the form of a categorical imperative' (Freud, 1923b, p. 35). We are born with the id—a body ego; the superego is acquired later and its legacies are many. It is the heir of the id and also the heir of the Oedipus complex, but for the latter to take place, it must wait for the death or the dissolution of the Oedipus complex.

The superego contains within it a structure of the socio-cultural world. It is the precipitate of the psychic assimilation of many conflicting mandates, duties, and admonishments. Morality, culture, and history all leave their mark upon it. Religion, education, and authority (Freud, S. 1923b, p. 35) all play a part in its make-up. The benign aspect of the superego brings the human being nearer to the elevated psychic functions related to the sublimation of drives whereas its negative side is allied to sadism due to anal regression, the result of the frustration of libidinal impulses. It is here that destructive impulses reside, and evil finds a vehicle through which it can be manifested. Murderous impulses are supported by rationalizations. The destructive urge becomes a strong imperative, be it conscious or unconscious.

The superego has a number of important functions in psychoanalytic treatment which focuses on the positive dimension:

a. It acts as a guardian. By means of the prohibition, sublimation and the repression of ego impulses, it contributes to the taming of drives, resulting in mental harmony.
b. It is a mental organizer, bringing to the psyche a sense of law, order and social norms (the paternal function).
c. It is an inner voice which quietly urges the attainment of a state of well-being. The small (at times almost inexistent), element of sadism present in the superego enables the development of an intense life-force. Unconscious mandates pave the way to a state of psychic well-being. Even when confronted by life's vicissitudes, the superego tries to make the best of a difficult situation.

The superego is not only a guardian of the psyche but is also the propitiator of resolutions and decisions that help to attenuate feelings of suffering and malaise.

CHAPTER THREE

Clinical work and positivity

Introduction

The analytical space is one in which there exists an interplay of environmental and psychosomatic factors, where flows of energy and lines of force exist between analyst and analysand, and where spatial, temporal and geographical dimensions interconnect. It is the domain of different functions where diverse phenomenal factors combine. Its complexity derives from that which is inherent in the psychoanalytical process itself. Freud (1905a [1904]) said that, 'For it is not so easy to play upon the instrument of the mind' (p. 262). The essential ambiguity of the analytical situation (Baranger, M. & Baranger, W. 1961–1962) demands a great degree of plasticity on the part of the psychoanalyst.

The analyst's work takes place in the midst of torments and conflicts. The painful sessions in which pathology and its unconscious roots are explored can be likened to an operation with insufficient anaesthetic. The curative objective is to alleviate the psyche by means of the lifting of repressions and the resolution of pathogenic nuclei. By bringing unconscious, intolerable representations into the conscious, the subject—by means of working-through—is freed of symptomatic complexes and is able to build a psychic space with a greater inner freedom, a side effect of which is a sense of well-being.

However, this does not mean that psychoanalysis has to be serious, quasi-solemn, or what could be termed 'ill-humoured'[1] Certain rituals of the psychoanalytical setting from past decades (the poker-face when welcoming the patient, exaggerated neutrality, little gesturing, stern expression) add little to the efficacy of the treatment. These were mannerisms from a certain era which were presumed to lead to greater rigour. This seriousness and rigidity in the psychoanalytical setting were in the service of a technical ideal, and not always in the service of treating the patient.

Throughout history, psychoanalysis has been the object of cultural conditioning and of power struggles between different factions. Adherence to an ideology was hidden behind the pretext of science. What took place was a tendency to de-idealize and to relativize. Creativity became an imperative, serving to challenge established ideas and to surmount obstacles which hindered the furtherance of knowledge. When analysis proved boring or insipid (Blanton, S. 1930), the analyst's work was ineffective consequent not only of their blind spots but also their lack of professional skills.

The job of the analyst operates both in the darkness of a tragic hell and in the inner space of freedom and mental harmony. Even in extreme situations when tragedy invades the psyche, there exists a safe haven, a place which is life-sustaining in the midst of the residue of unbearable pain.

The analyst keeps this place within sight, no matter how small. It is this minute fragment of the psyche which remains separate from that which is sick or has been damaged.

The analytical process has limits (Freud, S. 1893a). Freud, for example, stated that neurasthenia is not analysable. The broadening of the scope of psychoanalytical method and its application in new fields such as psychosis, family and couples therapy and in psychosomatic pathology has modified the psychoanalytical setting and the classical or orthodox idea of 'what should be done'.

---

[1]Julio Campos. This refers to an expression used during his presentation in the VIII Conference of the Psychoanalytical Society of Rio Grande do Sul, *Eros and Solitude*, Porto Alegre, April 1999.

Unexplored pathways have been opened up and new criteria have emerged in terms of what can and cannot be analysed.

The analytical field is now an open field of knowledge which leaves room for new discoveries and potential paradigms.

The factors which intervene in transference—counter-transference—can be divided into verbal and non-verbal. They delimit spaces which, on the one hand, are wordless, and, on the other, are interpretative-enunciative.

In phenomenological terms, they can be categorized in the following way: unconscious transmission, body–body interchanges between patient and analyst, the maintenance of the setting, and the bond between patient and analyst. These elements function at coexistent or alternative levels.

This widening of the psychoanalytical domain, reflected by the proliferation of different analytical schools of thought, accounts for its intrinsic complexity and its inevitable relativization. The different theories of the psychoanalytical process, with their multiplicity of variables and paucity of invariables, demonstrate the difficulty which exists in trying to be sure of the correct interpretation, the precise iatrogenic or curative effect of an intervention and so on and so forth.

Psychoanalytic research investigates and verifies hypotheses and criteria for validation. Because of its inexactness, psychoanalysis allows the microscope to observe only a part of the process. The part which is ineffable and imprecise, which cannot be accurately measured or categorized, means that it is inevitable that psychoanalysis is a discipline which has a unique, personalized, 'crafted' quality where ethics, responsibility and the skills of every professional play a part.

The positive dimension of psychoanalytical work requires the consideration of certain technical premises. This also applies to psychotherapists with an analytical orientation.

There is an inherent positivity in psychoanalytical work.

The first positive step is taken in the encounter between the analyst's passion to analyse, and the desire of the analysand to be analysed.

Ethics feature from the outset with the commitment on the part of the analyst to treat the patient, the prior evaluation of their empathy for the patient, and their acceptance of the responsibility inherent in the analytical task.

The handling of empathetic boundaries becomes the first tool. Treatment with a new patient should not be initiated if the analyst finds this rationally or emotionally unacceptable due to their own life story. Freud (1895d) said: 'I cannot imagine bringing myself to delve into the psychical mechanism of a hysteria in anyone who struck me as low-minded and repellent, and who, on closer acquaintance, would not be capable of arousing human sympathy' (p. 265). Thus some technical postulates of analysis include an element of positivity.

Catharsis, with its ensuing discharge from the complex of representations and affects linked to a painful event, leads to a lightening of the psychic load. Abreaction adds words, at some time or another, to the pathogenic history of a patient. The abreactive model can be likened to the satisfying of an urgent bodily need, and is an evacuative model of a certain peremptory nature. The words which were contained are released and flow out, bringing relief.

Containment eases the suffering of a patient by recreating a protective function in the psychoanalytical field of the session. The work of free association seeks to contribute to the task of increasing those positive inner spaces. I will quote Freud (1893a) once again, who said:

> 'Abreaction', however, is not the only method of dealing with the situation that is open to a normal person who has experienced a psychical trauma. A memory of such a trauma, even if it has not been abreacted, enters the *great complex of associations*,[2] it comes alongside other experiences, which may contradict it, and is subjected to rectification by other ideas. After an accident, for instance, the memory of the danger and the (mitigated) repetition of the fright becomes associated with a memory of what happened afterwards—rescue and the consciousness of present safety. Again, a person's memory of a humiliation is corrected by his [*sic*] putting the facts right, by *considering*[3] his [*sic*] own worth, etc. In this way a normal person is able to bring about the disappearance of the accompanying affect through the process of association (p. 9).

---

[2]My emphasis.
[3]My emphasis.

The work of the analyst is to explore these representations (reflections) which rectify a traumatic memory by linking traumatic representations with non-traumatic representations.

Free association, the classic requisite of analytical work, is an ideal which many times the analysand only succeeds in reaching at the end of the treatment. This is influenced by a multiplicity of factors, both conscious and unconscious: by resistance, submission to the analyst, barriers of disgust, shame and embarrassment and so on. When the *great complex of associations* is called upon, there is nothing to prevent the psychoanalyst from helping to promote the movement of memory traces.

The taming of trauma (Baranger, M., Baranger, W. & Mom, J.M. 1988) and its working-through are two principal chapters of the theory of psychoanalytical technique.

The taming of trauma—by means of historization—enables tragedy to be symbolized, adding symbolic representations and affects to the patient's history. This historization or *temporary retraumatizing,* which is vital for the dissolution of trauma, must be undertaken with skill, subtlety and great care. Trauma is revisited with the aim of neutralizing the traumatizing power of the unconscious. This point begs an interesting question: what are the limits of the historization of trauma? Is it not too ambitious or hopeful to believe that it is possible to historize a trauma effectively in its entirety? This point is given consideration in the section of the book related to the iatrogenic effect of traumatization.

Working-through is another fundamental aspect in treatment. This process, which is typically slow, arduous and difficult and which depends on the previous pathology of the patient, coexists with the process of historization and symbolization. When working-through is successful, pain and acute suffering are transformed by means of an internal mutation into self-knowledge. This is particularly the case in the mourning process.

Unconscious transmission

Freud (1915e) describes unconscious transmission between different individuals and gives this the category of 'a given'. He does not go more deeply into this subject in his meta-psychological theorizing nor does he specify the intervening variables. The existence of this phenomenon is indubitable and is proven by experience. He writes:

> It is a very remarkable thing that the *Ucs.* of one human being cannot react upon that of another, without passing through the *Cs.* This deserves closer investigation, especially with a view to finding out whether preconscious activity can be excluded as playing a part in it; but, descriptively speaking, that fact is incontestable (p. 194).

He had given an example of this phenomenon two years previously where a woman, unable to have children because of her husband, fell ill at seeing her hopes of motherhood shattered. She endeavoured to hide her frustration and inner conflict from her husband. Freud (1913i) says:

> But I have good reason for asserting that everyone possesses in his [*sic*] own unconscious an instrument with which he [*sic*] can interpret the utterances of the unconscious in other people. Her husband understood, without any admission or explanation on her part, what his wife's anxiety meant (p. 320).

This *instrument* occupies a central place in the analytical field. The unconscious of the analyst and of the patient are subtly intertwined, which enables the perception of subliminal messages, the prevention of destructive acting-outs, the understanding of complex dynamics, along with the intuition of affects and representations. The analysis of the analyst themselves paves the way to a greater permeability with their own unconscious, a process which proves its worth in the consulting room.

Transmission between the unconscious of different individuals is a phenomenon which has only been partially elucidated.

The psychic space which is created by the transmission between the unconscious of different individuals is referred to in the following affirmation of M. and W. Baranger (1961–1962): 'Our technique, in part, highlights the magic of the word.' In this 'magic' is anchored that which cannot be formalized by the common categories of logic.

This interweaving of the unconscious arising from the analytical dialogue between both protagonists becomes transformed into a rather unusual game of chess (Freud, S. 1913c). Unconscious transmission can be verbalized or can be wordless.

When the analyst is distracted and loses their floating attention, they 'betray' the task at hand.[4] Floating attention is paradoxical as it requires a balance of concentration and distraction on the part of the analyst.

The blind spots, counter-transferential obstacles and private conflicts of the analyst can cause a lack of analytical focus and disrupt the course of the treatment.

Transformative impetus

By 'transformative impetus' I refer to a set of strategies and technical premises which are aimed at achieving certain objectives in the curative process. Although a total cure is an impossible objective, every responsible analyst is focused on the goal of attenuating the pathology and improving the mental health of the patient.

This strange, inexact science called psychoanalysis requires the blending of both knowledge and art. The art derives from the creativity and the skill of the analyst, and from the ability to bring the unconscious into play. What is more, the knowledge is fluid, in a state of movement and not exempt from surprises and partial modifications, which open the door to new conceptualizations.

This transformative impetus steers the dynamic of the therapeutic, bonding process and may be discontinuous. Owing to the fact that it is exposed to numerous vicissitudes, its trajectory is neither linear nor predetermined. The body, chance, catastrophes, knowledge, all influence the potential for psychic change.

'Transformative impetus' is a term which expresses activity, activity which is generated in the interchange between analyst and patient in a relationship which is both spoken and unspoken, and which is at the same time between two and/or multiple real or imaginary inhabitants of a shared psychic world. The work of analysis is related to action. This is not at odds with the rule of abstinence or the immobility of the patient on the divan. The analyst focuses their efforts on their goal 'without precipitation and without pausing',

[4]R Sciarreta. Personal communication (1980).

surmounting obstacles, overcoming resistances, unhindered by impasses. An analysis without risks and without fear is an analysis which is paralysed. The classic or orthodox techniques and strategies serve as a reference point from which the skill and the personal spontaneity of each analyst begins to develop. It is maybe because of this that Freud (1913c), on many occasions, said that his technical principles should not be followed to the letter. With these words, he encouraged the spirit of creativity and investigation in psychoanalysis, paving the way for future advances.

This transformative process must not overlook the physical dimension of bodily 'presence' in the analytical dyad, which plays a crucial part in psychoanalytical work.

I will consider diverse factors which are part of this process, namely: interpretation, the presence of the analyst, working with an open door, the study and comprehension of clinical material and the role of the insignificant.

Interpretation

An interpretation is a group of words articulated with the intention of producing a liberating effect on the psyche. It takes the form of an attempt to communicate with the unconscious. Silence, a non-verbal form of expression, can also serve the function of interpreting. However, the verbal medium occupies a privileged place in the art of interpreting.

The rigour of interpretation has already been analysed in minute detail.

A certain zeal for interpretive perfection can be deduced from some conceptualizations in this aspect of psychoanalytical work. The analyst's intention to mutate and transform requires a type of Gestaltic structure and takes place in stages (Strachey, J. 1934). A complete interpretation[5] is fundamental for producing a psychic change: it must highlight the point of urgency of the conflict along with the resistance, the defence mechanism and the transferential element which is being worked on.

The analyst's words may be idealized by the patient. These words, which are idealized and which also make demands on the

[5] Achaval, J. (1972). Personal communication.

patient, erode interpretive spontaneity and *the necessary ignorance* of the interchange between the unconscious of the analyst and of the patient. It is difficult to measure the dosage of interpretive rigour and interpretive freedom in an analytical formulation. There is as yet no consensus of opinion regarding this matter and discussions have tended to be inconclusive.

The study of clinical material reveals many different forms of verbal interchange between the psychoanalyst and the patient: questions, statements which are framed hypothetically, shared information, comments, and suggestions (Etchegoyen, H. 1999).

Diversity is the salient feature in this scenario. From sessions where little is said, where words are chosen with great care and precision, to more talkative sessions in which the work of 'transference neurosis' alternates with the non-transference relationship (Greenson, R. & Wexler, M. 1969). Each analytical apprentice makes their mistakes. Given that the training period is interminable, a certain feeling of 'failure' in the analyst is inevitable, even when experience and common sense reduce the number of errors made.

When we consider the function of interpretation, there is a consensus that it consists of 'making the unconscious conscious', which produces a liberating effect. This liberation is achieved by means of a) the lightening of the psychic load and b) a psychic excision.

a. The lightening of the psychic burden requires working-through. This process involves the resolution of pathogenic complexes on the one hand and working with the patient's health on the other.
b. The psychic excision consists of 'letting fall' a sick nucleus. By means of working-through and catharsis, the patient arrives at a psychic 'enough is enough!' which enables them to free themselves from a problem which not only caused suffering but which was also the cause of great libidinal retention. The patient succeeds in dominating their past and ventures into new areas of psychic functioning.

Making the unconscious conscious and producing a liberating effect are not interdependent. Frequently, it can be observed that 'making conscious the unconscious' does not produce the expected outcome from the process of working-through. The 'instantaneous liberating effect' of some interpretations is not due to their content but rather to the meta-verbal influence of the word-voice of the analyst who, in transference, becomes a supportive and protective object. The patient's suffering is alleviated temporarily. The sessions prove beneficial to the patient as they constitute a form of psychic 'sustenance' which attenuates feelings of helplessness and archaic anxieties caused by certain life experiences. In addition, the patient may succeed in carrying out the interpretation-order or interpretation-wish of the analyst, with the aim of gaining—by means of submission—the approval and love of the analyst.

The interpretation possesses a certain degree of ineffability. The way in which working-through and the cure comes about is not always the result of representation or interpretative formalization. Many words, carefully chosen, lack a transformative effect. Nothing guarantees or explains systematically when an interpretation reaches those strata of the unconscious and triggers the process of working-through and psychic change. This mystery is one of the challenges of interpretation.

The domain of the meta-verbal and the non-verbal have an influence on the effectiveness of interpretations. The tone of voice, physical appearance and gestures convey information from both the analyst and the patient. The interpretation carries with it a bodily, physical aspect—the voice is something physical—and an affective aspect. Isolating a word for the sake of it being a mere word is an academic exercise and does not reflect material or psychic reality.

The interpersonal space created between analyst and patient in the analytical field creates a network of interpretations, which, in turn, are interpreted by the patient and many times thrown back into the analyst's court like a sort of *interpretative game*. The analytical dyad constructs interpretations together which complete and/or correct and transform the initial interpretation. This working in unison enriches the analysis by giving it a dynamic quality. Analytical listening includes the interpretation of the patient and the patient's understanding of this interpretation.

Not every rejection of an interpretation is due to resistance on the part of the analysand. Patients tend to anticipate the course of interpretation.

I remember a young borderline patient who displayed anti-social behaviour. I interpreted a self-destructive acting-out such that it was experienced by the patient like a condemnation from the superego.

The patient said to me: 'Not in that way, not like that.' "This interpretation", which was both a sign and a warning, successfully steered the course of the treatment in the direction of the cure.

There are no set rules which distinguish the correct interpretation from the incorrect interpretation. The validation of an interpretation is seen in the outcome of the treatment during the psychoanalytical process.

Only the course of treatment, those experiences and ideas which surface in both the inner and external worlds of the patient, and the consolidation of changes over time, will provide evidence of changes which are the result of working-through, and which can profoundly transform the psyche.

Presence and person: La via di porre

Interpretation, the fundamental task in psychoanalysis, is complemented by the presence of the analyst. Nacht (1962) even gave a greater value to 'presence' than to interpretation. In referring to this, she says:

> It is this deep inner attitude which, in my opinion, is a decisive factor, and that is why I have often maintained that it is what the analyst *is* rather than what he *says* that matters. It is this "presence" which will determine, for example, the modification of the superego, the process of identification, and above all the minimizing of the subject's habitual ambivalence (p. 207, emphasis in the original).

The mere presence of the analyst generates a positive quantum of energy which is both conscious and unconscious, priming the analyst to understand and bond with the patient. The vitality of the analyst, their history and their position in the face of unhappiness and suffering is brought into play. The analysis of the analyst, their periodic reanalysis and their passion for the science of analysis play a part in this presentification. Lacan (1964 p. 113–122) said that the very presence of the analyst is a manifestation of the unconscious. Transference emanates from the analyst as does their sincere desire to analyse.

The vitality of interpretation, which is conveyed via intonation and the presence of the analyst, plays a role in producing certain effects in the unconscious of the patient.

The idea that the analyst acts *per via de levare* and not *per via de porre* cannot be generalized. The analyst gives their energy, their communicative skills, their capacity for empathy, their opinion and inevitably their ideology. This act of 'giving' interacts with the discourse of the patient and influences the progress of the curative process.

Interpretive purity is an ideal which is both asymptotic and imperfect. *La via de levare* is allied to *la via de porre*. The 'being' of the analyst needs to be explored analytically to gain a better understanding of what psychic consequences their personality produces in the treatment of their patients. Analytical neutrality, the analyst 'without memory and without desire', the function of a blank page for the patient's projections and transferences, the cold and efficient surgeon, are expressions and ideals which are useful insofar as they order and systematize different strands of the theory behind psychoanalytical technique, but are in fact useless and false when they are endowed with the quality of absolute truth.

The delicate analytical task operates both *per via di levare*, with respect to that which concerns lifting repressions, and *per via de porre*, with respect to that which relates to the influence which the presence of the analyst exerts and their specific way of working.

It is necessary to make a distinction between the analyst as a good person and as an effective professional. Freud considered the analysis of each analyst to be of prime importance for those who wanted to follow the profession. Transference and counter-transference move delicate threads which put to the test the analytical skill of plumbing the depths of the resistances and symptoms of the analysand. Factors which are very personal and relate to skill, ability and individual sagacity are brought into play. These factors cannot be explained solely by the number of hours one has studied or the academic qualifications held. Given that psychoanalysis is a discipline which has developed between the fields of art and science, a good psychoanalyst will be a good scientist-artist.

The mental health of the psychoanalyst will impact on their ability to set in motion the process of transformation. Excessive narcissism is one of the great obstacles facing the analyst; the desire for power is another impediment, along with authoritarianism and the analyst's use of charm and self-idealization to avoid losing patients.

Analytical practice cannot be limited to being the source of good intentions. The healing process, when only motivated by love, creates its own complexity and obliges us to study its fallacies. Love, when directed towards a patient, can mask latent feelings of hostility or a pathogenic analytical perspective if commiseration for the suffering individual is given great importance.

The patient can perceive whether what they have said is thought to be of value from the way the analyst looks in a session, just as they can perceive whether the analyst is interested or bored.

Freud (1937c) wrote: 'Among the factors which influence the prospects of analytic treatment and add to its difficulties in the same manner as the resistances, must be reckoned not only the nature of the patient's ego but the individuality of the analyst' (p. 247).

The patient who tends to be healthy wants his or her analyst to be positive—'alive'—in every session. The implication of this Winicottian expression is that the psychoanalyst makes a commitment with respect to their own life-force. The 'psychic death' of the analyst, the moments of being in a psychically moribund state (Alizade, M. 1995), limits their therapeutic skill: the desire to analyse weakens, the counter-transferential process becomes stagnant and neurotic, and the ability to listen diminishes. The presence of the analyst ceases to serve its analytical function. If the patient has an unconscious hatred of life[6], the excessive vitality of the analyst will exacerbate their feelings of hostility and negative transference.

In psychoanalysis, the rigorous and the ineffable are at opposite poles and it is a balance between the two that the analyst strives to achieve. Interpretation is an instrument which is both powerful and vulnerable. The transformative impetus employs both tried and tested techniques and others which are also very effective even though they have not been theoretically formalized.

The future of psychoanalysis will be enriched with the findings from research, which will contribute to the furtherance of knowledge.

---

[6]'Unconscious hatred of life' is an expression used by Ch Bollas. This was mentioned during a discussion after his presentation in one of the conferences of the Argentine Psychoanalytical Association to refer to an unconscious affect of a person who adheres excessively to social conventions.

Working with an open door

Every session forms part of a long process which unfolds over the passage of time and which also takes place in an isolated, unique timeframe. The latter is a reconfirmation of the patient's choice to continue analysis, a choice which is repeated session after session. The patient repeatedly makes a choice to continue their treatment. This repeated choice has various meta-psychological registers: it can be unconsciously ignored by the patient, it can be overtly expressed by means of positive or negative transference, or it can be resisted silently until a threshold is reached resulting in a negative therapeutic reaction.

The analyst always retains their ethical stance: their wish is to analyse the patient who has agreed to be in analysis but they do not attempt to retain the patient by making use of the authority which their position may give them. The door is open; that is to say, the patient comes to a session of his or her own volition with the least possible pressure on the part of the analyst. The patient is guided by their enthusiasm and the relief that they feel by being surrounded by positivity generated in the sessions as well as their strong desire to understand themselves better with the aim of alleviating their suffering. The patient is also guided by habit and at times a type of submission to, or dependence on, the analyst.

The analyst is responsible for keeping the door open. From the first interviews, the analyst should not be worried about whether the patient will or will not begin treatment, and in the worst situations, when, in the middle of the psychoanalytical process a storm of hatred is unleashed—due to a negative therapeutic reaction—the door should still remain open.

This concept of the open-door does not exclude the idea of a protective covering of positivity but it does determine its permeability and containment. Treatment will prove iatrogenic if the analyst takes an authoritarian approach, suffocating the patient and forcing them into submission by taking advantage of the weakness of the patient's ego or the analyst's idealized position. Freedom is of prime importance when treating a patient.

It can be argued that the patient is always right when they complain, demanding more attention and better results. Resistance is not at the root of everything. Common sense must be used in response to the protests of a patient dissatisfied with the progress of their treatment.

The analyst, freed of sterile narcissism, accepts their limits. At times, the patient cannot work through their problems, or there is no favourable outcome, or the relationship between analyst and patient does not gel. Within the framework of failure, the analyst continues with the interminable learning process. If, in the analyst's mind, the door is always open, the threat of the interruption of a patient is transformed into an interesting challenge. When this does not threaten the prestige or self-esteem of the analyst, this can be investigated with calmness, intelligence and enthusiasm. The ethical commitment of the analyst cannot be left aside.

Working with an open door has the following characteristics:

1. An atmosphere of containment and of working without restraints.
2. A feeling of openness or the predominance of a benevolent superego.
3. The patient's perception that the analyst neither wishes to keep them in analysis nor is worried about their leaving.
4. Basic mutual trust: the analyst allows the patient's 'coming' and 'going'. The progression of hate-love-reparation is able to flow unhindered.
5. The demand flows and is an integral part of the analytical process.
6. The frequent reiteration of the demand. The patient chooses their analyst many times in the midst of the clamour of the analytical process.

Clinical vignette

R, a young patient, wished to reduce the number of sessions after two years of analysis; the process had got close to touching certain important resistant nuclei. The analyst considered that if the frequency of sessions was reduced, the treatment would run the risk of becoming ineffective. The analyst pressed the patient to keep the same number of weekly sessions. The patient was then absent many times, ringing to cancel sessions. From R's case history, we can extract the following information: the patient was hyper-stimulated sexually with many different forms of bodily contact in her childhood. She slept in the same bed between both of her parents until adolescence. Her mother smothered her with kisses, this being a mixture of affection and aggression. In her puberty, R's older brother fondled her genitals repeatedly. Her memories are vague. R became very distressed and distanced herself emotionally from the analyst when referring to this subject.

In the transference, this attempt to escape from a closed, endogamic environment was re-edited. This feeling of being enclosed was repeated in the transference. When the analyst 'opened the door' and stopped pressurizing the patient to come to the sessions, the defence mechanism was acknowledged and the analytical atmosphere was modified. Not only did R go to the sessions regularly but soon after expressed her desire to increase the frequency of sessions.

R explicitly demonstrated that there exists a distinction between the analyst who understands their patient and the analyst who criticizes their patient. The analyst here occupied both places: in the past, the analyst demanded that the patient came to the session (criticism) and now understands and values them despite their resistances.

The analysis continued and work began on the traumatic nuclei of early seduction.

The study of clinical material

Clinical material refers to the text, usually written, which narrates the complexity of the life history of a patient during the initial interviews and over the course of the sessions. It can be expressed in oral form, as a live commentary of the interchange between analyst and patient. It is a written record which serves as evidence of the analyst's diagnosis and prognosis, and the progress of the treatment. The analyst details various diagnoses (psychopathological, the degree of analysability), a prognosis deriving from the first diagnostic impression, and a prognosis over the course of the trial period of treatment.

The clinical material is used as the raw material for the later working-through both on an individual level as well as in the context of group supervision, the aim of which is to reach a deeper understanding of the semiology of the case history being studied and to achieve a better clinical outcome.

The reading of clinical material results in the analyst working with one or more qualified professionals.

Different aspects of the clinical material are studied such as pathogenic factors, defence mechanisms, identifications, the effects of deprivation at an early age and narcissistic disturbances. Tragic stories are recounted, concatenations of traumatic events are examined, and adverse factors in the complemental series are analysed.

The profession of the psychoanalyst is considered to be an extremely unhealthy one by virtue of the fact that the psyche of the analyst is constantly stimulated by catastrophic and threatening events.

Clinical material always has a certain bias as it is impossible for the analyst to be divorced from theories, ideas and professional prejudices. Analytical effectiveness is improved when the analyst succeeds in putting aside preconceived ideas and value judgements.

The analysis of clinical material has both psychopathological and ideological aspects. Social prejudices form part of the thinking apparatus of the analyst in an almost natural way and are thus practically unavoidable. The analyst needs to work on their self-awareness in terms of what they consider to be acceptable and what they are averse to. Many is the time that ideological assumptions impregnate theory with preconceived notions which render psychoanalytic listening less effective, and as a consequence fundamentally hinder operative efficacy. For example, the analyst may take sides with a member of their patient's family, may criticize a specific relational aspect or negatively judge the sexual conduct of their patient. The convictions of the analyst as regards the traumatic value of an event influence the way in which the problem will be resolved.

A sort of professional 'deformation' is rife in our discipline. As a result of being immersed in traumas and conflicts to such a degree, the analyst tends to undervalue the healthy part of the psyche which the patient has managed to preserve, preferring to focus their energies on exploring concealed memories and reconstructing tragic scenarios.

The valuing of the patient in their entirety implies a profound acceptance of their life history.

The existing emotions and representations of the patient, their life history and its development should be seen, in the first instance, as if they were mere belongings of the subject who comes for treatment. In the macro context of the patient's life, the narrative of events is separated from moral connotations. The patient is taken for what they *are*: the product of an interlinking of their personal diachrony and synchrony. The analyst tries to shed their self, discarding their preconceived notions so that they can increase their understanding of the analysand. Their listening becomes neutral yet at the same time emotionally charged and they endeavour to separate their floating attention from their inevitable prejudices.

When the discourse of the patient becomes incompatible with the ideology of the analyst, the analyst must perform a self-analysis of the counter-transferential effects to avoid acting-out and should consider the possibility of eventually referring the patient to another colleague.

It is not unusual to hear derogatory comments against a 'bad mother' or 'bad father' when examining clinical material. In the case of psychotic patients, it is usually the mother who gets bad press. On other occasions, the analysis of clinical material arouses expressions of condolence and commiseration bordering on what Dolto called 'pathogenic pity' (1982, p. 210) and what could be termed 'worthless sympathy'. The pathology of this attitude lies in the fact that it may mask hostile feelings and diminish the analyst's interest in the patient, who is considered to be a hopeless case.

Example a: An analyst with religious convictions condemned a priori their patient's abortion, thus intensifying the patient's feelings of guilt.

Example b: An analyst considers that their female patient has a negative, phallic attitude as they do not want children.

An examination of the clinical case history of each patient shows that, in both of the above cases, owing to the moral stance of the analyst, the patient was perceived as having a pathological problem.

Example c: An analyst condemns the infidelity of a patient's husband and urges her to get a divorce.

The patient perceives the wishes and the will of the analyst. They may try to please the analyst to win their love and acceptance, at the expense of behaving artificially by mimicking aspects of a false self. The patient's unconscious perception of the analyst's lack of confidence in achieving a positive outcome may trigger a latent depression and may result in the interruption of treatment.

From the perspective of positivity, the study of clinical material must focus on what is given and on what the patient 'is', with minimal value judgements. Thereafter, the psychopathology can unfold in an environment in which the dynamic is one of understanding and open psychoanalytical listening. This attitude requires that the analyst perceives negative counter-transference in order to analyse it and transform it into a tool which can be used in the analytical process. The role of the analyst, in their professional capacity, is neither to condemn nor to pass judgement but rather to enable the patient's life story and the resultant clinical material to flow freely into their 'laboratory' for further investigation. This investigation of a case history and the desire to achieve therapeutic efficacy are the challenges which the psychoanalyst faces and it is here that the passion for analysis develops. This ideal objective is only ever achieved imperfectly and asymptotically.

The role of insignificance

This can be understood as the incorporation into analytical listening and clinical work of everything which fits into the category of the insignificant: happenings, gestures, acts, thoughts and so on.

From the vantage point of positivity, the insignificant stands out in stark relief and is of vital importance. Since it neither responds to ideals nor pressure from the superego, it consists of all that which is free from judgements and self-criticism. The insignificant makes up a field which is essentially tranquil and peaceful. Everyday insignificant events are relevant in that they quieten the mind and teach us—for those who choose to learn—about our existence and the value of accepting the relativity of everything that happens in life.

The struggle against insignificance has resulted in numerous victims. Equating insignificance with triviality is to ignore the role that it plays in healthy mental functioning. The neurotic feels beset by self-imposed demands and unrealistic ideals, and consequently pays the price: morbid psychic tension which predisposes them to illness and life-long suffering.

Theoretical and technical tools

I will describe certain key elements in this approach.

Silence

> The toil and trouble, father, that I bore
> To find thy lodging-place and how thou faredst,
> I spare thee; surely 'twere a double pain
> To suffer, first in act and then in telling;
> — Ismene in Sophocles' *Oedipus in Colonos*

In contrast to the defence mechanisms of the unconscious ego, this defence mechanism is largely preconscious/conscious. The patient realizes that recounting is reliving, and that remaining silent is forgetting. Words reopen old wounds, while silence becomes a balm.

To keep a tragedy silent is a way of keeping a respectful distance from defence mechanisms when faced with the pain of unbearable memories. This mechanism of silence as a preconscious defence is a phenomenon I have previously discussed in a paper concerning the psychoanalytical treatment of dying patients (Alizade, 1995). Without words, death is named: with words, it is silenced. The painful representation of impending death and the final farewell to life is tolerated by keeping silent. In some cases, the name of death is only whispered.

When using silence as a curative tool, the analyst requires careful timing, and must be sensitive to the many signs which indicate the times and places when they should speak and what they should say and the occasions when they should keep quiet.

In cases in which the trauma has besieged the psyche in its entirety due to excessive traumatization (Gubrich-Simitis, 1979), the analyst must perform their surgery with great precision when dealing with any clinical material arising from the patient. Severely traumatized individuals may often prefer to keep silent as regards their past sufferings and will only venture to tell what they remember if they feel psychically protected and contained by their environment.

Silence will only be replaced by narration once the working bond between analyst and analysand has been cemented and the patient feels safe within a covering of positivity.

Silence increases the quantum of positivity since it protects the psyche from iatrogenic hyper-stimulation. We find here both a technical limit and a warning with respect to the basic assumption of psychoanalysis: 'Tell everything.'

The mechanism of silence provides an opening for the investigation of meta-verbal phenomena and the inclusion of the semiology of silence in psychoanalytic processes (Alizade, 1995, Chapter 8).

Vital silences should be distinguished from deathly ones (ibid.). The former are open, outwardly directed, and facilitate transmission from one unconscious system to another; the latter are closed, isolated, and impenetrable.

To the well-known Freudian 'talking cure' I would like to add the dimension of the 'silent cure' (ibid. p. 134).

In some cases, the semiology of silence leads us to think of words as a noise-screen hiding a silence which signifies a psychic void.

Psychical calm: Un-thinking

The tendency to excessive verbalization in treatment stems from the very constitution of psychoanalysis, which needs words to undo false links and thus bring about psychical change. But words are not all that there is, and very often, when an ideational complex short-circuits and the patient's redundant, repetitive discourse persists, words become an obstacle. In those circumstances, there is much talk but nothing is said. The mind is submerged in a kind of ideational rumination, a futile vicious circle preventing the free flow of associations, as if one associative pathway had taken possession of all the courses of thought. Masochistic pleasure plays a part in this extreme polarization towards this one complex which seems impossible to erode. Instead of reaching the depths of the unconscious, words do not break the surface and monotonously circle the same space, resulting in *representational excess*.

The nucleus of the conflict takes on an obsessive character and sessions can become a repetitious torturous ordeal. Nothing is resolved: the mind is beseiged by anxiety-provoking thoughts as if cornered in a psychical space with no way out. Sometimes, both patient and analyst build a bastion of resistances around this central recurring theme. Sessions reveal mental fatigue brought on by an excess of thinking accompanied by a lack of working-through with no psychic change. Putting an end to the representational and affective excess of the patient's psyche allows it to temporarily withdraw from the damage and the resulting impoverishment caused by this excess of representations.

This respite is both necessary and has positive effects. It is a healthy 'analytical impasse' that may last a whole session, half a session, or even just a few vivifying minutes. The analyst does not try to go deeper with their interpretations, realizing that this will only exacerbate a hyper-facilitated memory trace which continually discharges along the same pathway. An analogy would be that of the wheel of a car stuck fast in a muddy road, which sinks deeper and deeper when the driver accelerates.

When psychical calm is restored, the atmosphere of the analytic field gradually becomes free of the damaging excess of representations and new associative pathways are opened up.

The analyst contributes to the process of 'un-thinking', broadening its representational scope to other 'psychical zones'. They do not respond to the patient's continual revisiting of one particular theme and the goal of their interventions is the dissolution of this harmful nucleus. Thus the patient learns that the session may also have a more silent, relaxing function of transmitting a calm therapeutic empathy.

When the emotionally exhausted patient says: 'I always talk about the same things every session. I'm boring myself,' the analyst is given permission to deviate from the usual representational pathways and to encourage the patient and sustain them psychically in their mischievous, trivial, insignificant associations. Thus, the relevance of the role of *trophic insignificance* is clearly illustrated. The analyst and the patient agree to a truce in the analytic battle against illness. The process of un-thinking actively contributes to the patient's well-being.

The mind attempts to empty itself of all thoughts. Within silence, there is comfort. When calm descends, this serenity is accompanied by a playful, light-hearted dimension. The psyche is temporarily relieved of its neurosis and the experience of un-thinking undermines the psychic arsenal of negativity and morbidity.

Mental calm expands the realms of thinking, enabling creativity to thrive.

The covering of positivity

When referring to the beginning of a treatment, Freud wrote: "The first aim of any treatment is always to attach the patient to the cure and to the person of the physician" (Freud, 1913c, p. 139). The word *attach* (*attachieren* in the German original) is associated with the idea of 'attracting something to oneself', of establishing a close link or bond. This quotation suggests a double bond: on the one hand, with the analyst and on the other, with the cure. The energy emanating from the life-drive of each member of the psychoanalytic dyad is mutually binding, which is reflected in the continuity of psychoanalytical treatment. The strength of this bond makes it easier for the patient to weather the analytic storms.

I would like to highlight those features which characterize this bond which are present in the psychoanalytic field, and to examine their effects over the course of the treatment.

This process of bonding generates the critical linking points in the weft between analyst and analysand that will sustain the analytical process during difficult periods. In times of resistance, the analyst may be put in check but the weft does not break because it is held together by the cure-object. When the patient's negative transference is unleashed on the analyst, the goal of the treatment is kept in sight. Thus the dyadic bond remains intact and the progress of the treatment is sustained. The analytic bond is often forced to surmount difficult traumatic obstacles.

From the patient's inner world emerge all the characters from their life history; the analyst sustains an 'inner group' of memories, scenes, fantasies, and desires.

The empathy of the analyst acts as a soothing, protective, surround. What develops is a psychical skin shared by analyst and patient in the interior of which those psychical connections damaged by past suffering are re-established. At this point, it is necessary to consider the non-transferential relationship with the analyst (Greenson, R. & Wexler, M. 1969; Etchegoyen, 1986, p. 219). This is a space where there is a simple, human communicative interchange between analyst and analysand, which plays a vital restorative role. The personality of both participants delimits an area that cannot be therapeutically formalized but which is crucial to the development of the curative process.

Didier Anzieu added the concept of 'covering' to psychoanalysis. On reviewing the scope of this term in Freud's work (Anzieu, 1990b, pp. 29–31), he observes that Freud's model is concerned with the boundaries between the psychical systems of an individual's mental apparatus. An extra layer of complexity was added to this model when Anzieu introduced the relational aspect and described a membrane structure with two faces, one turned to the outside world (a protective barrier against an influx of harmful stimuli) and the other to the inner world (the function of inscribing sensations and significations).

As has already been highlighted, an unconscious valence exists in the atmosphere of the consulting room where the pre-verbal and the sensual-affective acquire pre-eminence in the protective surround formed between analyst and patient.

Throughout the course of the sessions, verbal and non-verbal interaction gradually creates a protective covering where manifest elements (the positive therapeutic reaction, overt rejection) are interwoven with latent elements (unconscious transmission, empathy, and so on).

During the session, the psychical covering becomes a form of subtle membrane that has many dimensions and which takes multiple forms over the course of the analytical treatment. Sometimes it is a skin shared by analyst and patient, while at other times it is a shield-bastion involving both protagonists. This covering has a 'nomadic' quality (Anzieu, 1990b) and is an energy which flows within the space of the consulting room surrounding and covering bodies and parts of the psyche, evoking different emotions and senses.

The negative therapeutic reaction, counter-transferential hatred and perverse elements of the patient's personality all impact on this covering of positivity to different degrees according to each particular case. Although this protective psychic covering is governed by the life-drive, in its interior many tragic scenes are played out. Driven by the Thanatic aspects of their illness, the patient often encloses the psychic bond between analyst and analysand within a mortiferous covering of negativity made up of resistances, unconscious guilt, and sado-masochistic pleasure. The analyst struggles to neutralize this destructive force by endeavouring to overlay a new covering of positivity to regenerate the life-force of the patient. The patient's drive to create this covering is bound up with their life-instinct (Alizade, 1992 [1999]) and interwoven with the drive to attach a connective process which is an essential tool for the analyst in their treatment. When analysis comes to an end, the patient has shed their skin, and is healed, having recovered from the psychic damage caused by internal conflicts.

The patient's rejection of this protective psychic covering may take different forms: absences, a lack of acceptance of a high frequency of sessions, and so on. What the patient is rejecting, in actual fact, is the 'shared skin' of the relationship between analyst and patient, which necessitates constant visual, oral, and coenesthetic contact. In the majority of cases, this rejection is a defence mechanism against early experiences of damage or destruction of this protective surround with the primary object. The patient unconsciously fears that these painful experiences will reoccur and chooses withdrawal and detachment as a defence mechanism. Sometimes a long period of preanalysis is needed before the patient is able to tolerate the protective surround which provides the framework of the sessions, and can truly begin analysis.

I would now like to describe the psychic consequences which derive from the creation of this protective covering of positivity. It serves the following functions:

1. A protective screen in the analytical setting against an excess of excitation thus enabling the damaging effects of harmful stimuli to be minimized.
2. An atmosphere of emotional containment which provides a psychic refuge.
3. A mechanism which facilitates the establishment or strengthening of an inner 'rock core' providing psychic stability (Alizade, 1992 [1999], Chapter 2).
4. An inner space of waiting and trusting.
5. A protective shield which reflects the solidarity and support of others.
6. A covering which protects the patient from hatred and other negative feelings.

7. A covering that allows the patient to expose their narcissistic wounds, psychic scars, feelings of shame or disgust, the intimate world of daydreams and so forth.
8. A covering of intimacy.

De-dramatization

The kind of analysis I am proposing is one that tends to neutralize the force of tragedy, however intense this might be, thus creating an inner space of calm neutrality which will always be liberating and beneficial for the patient's well-being. This lightening of the psychic burden enables the patient to recover their libido, which had been previously consumed in futile suffering. The intensity of the life-drive is increased and channeled through the freed libido which is redeployed for the purpose of reparation and sublimation.

De-dramatizing refers to the minimization of the effects of a negative or tragic situation and requires decathexis and a reconsideration of pathogenic scenes. 'Reconsidering' signifies the creation of an alternative line of discourse which will enable the patient to modify their focus on conflict. This new focus requires a courageous and revolutionary reading of the facts that may disrupt roles which have been previously established. The patient must leave behind old prejudices, develop empathy for traumatogenic characters, overcome resentment which is chronically ingrained, and develop their potential to accept life's vicissitudes at a lighter, more playful level.

This process of refocusing enables the patient to invest less mental effort when reliving an inner conflict by neutralizing its harmful effects.

By relativizing the painful memory, it is put into perspective. The utilization of the principle of relativization when confronting traumatic facts reduces the intensity of negative feelings (hatred, fury, resentment, revenge, and so on). When inner turmoil diminishes, traumatic scenes take on a new dimension and are put into proportion. The deconstruction of destructiveness facilitates the gradual construction of a foundation of positivity.

The analyst's function is to act as the agent of the process of de-dramatization. However, in cases of extreme trauma, de-dramatization is slow and sometimes impossible.

Tangential interpretations

Tangential interpretation, a concept which I have explored previously (Alizade, 1995), is a technique which approaches points of conflict and resistance in a series of displacements which are metaphorical and metonymical. This demands a keen sense of timing on the part of the analyst, who must be sensitive to the patient's tolerance threshold. This form of interpretation works on the borders of the patient's defence mechanisms, in the same way as a tangent touches just one point of a curve. Thus the analyst can maintain the protective calm and can avoid triggering defence mechanisms when dealing with extremely painful events, such as the imminence of the patient's own death or that of a loved one.

Tangential interpretations serve as a measuring instrument, enabling the analyst to ascertain the patient's level of insight and permeability when making conscious the unconscious contents of their psyche.

Tangential interpretations may develop into a tangential psychic construction, eliciting a narrative from the patient or providing information about that which borders the painful representational-affective complex.

Creating psychic windows

Once it is clear that a constant interpretative focus on the same negative complex is unproductive, the analyst becomes the explorer of uncharted psychic territory, with the aim of finding new mental pathways and functions undiscovered in previous psychoanalytical treatment.

The creation of psychic windows—a term borrowed from the language of computers—requires that the psychoanalyst, using their knowledge and skill, takes an active approach. The realization that a seemingly valid interpretation proves ineffective impels the analyst to undertake an investigation of the patient's psyche, opening up new psychic spaces, insofar as the patient's psychopathology allows this. Questioning and building, a sort of *active archeological* approach, are the essential tools in this strategy. Through these new psychic windows, the analyst may glimpse hitherto unknown material.

The consolidation of positivity

Once the psychic burden is lightened and the mental functions that had been subjected to the harmful effects of the traumatic nucleus are restored, the healing process may begin.

Consolidation of positivity is an important analytic stage. The patient realizes that the healthy territory which has been recaptured must be fortified. Sessions take on an increasingly pleasant atmosphere, and the interlinking of memories, free from the turbulent past, has a peaceful quality. The patient's good humour increases, and enjoyment acquires the character of an objective which the patient actively wishes to achieve. This is not related to excessive or needless emotions, but rather to a harmonious, calm state of joyfulness.

The patient contributes to this process with interest, and even surprise. Happiness and the magic of sublimation and joy take on an analytic value per se, and are not just the consequence of the historization of pathological material. The patient learns that analysis not only attenuates neurotic suffering but also contributes to mental harmony. Inner peace has won the battle to claim a psychic space; a peaceful inner world is established.

This consolidation of positivity is a gradual process which takes place over the course of the sessions, and which intensifies in the latter stages of the treatment. The patient succeeds in changing their world view as regards the relative value they give both to neurotic suffering and to well-being. The daily task of learning to live a happy life and the cultivation of joyful insignificancies receive the positive support of the superego.

Limitations of clinical work and positivity

This approach is limited at several points in the psychoanalytic process, especially when symptoms intensify as a result of: 1) resistances and the negative therapeutic reaction, and 2) the patient 'hitting rock bottom' in their final attempt to hold on to their pathology before psychic change takes place, described by Freud (1895d [1893–1895]) as the last convulsion before the cure.

When this is the case, the positive dimension is concentrated in the work of the analyst, who must wait for the propitious moment to re-activate a positive perspective in the patient.

Some of the clinical situations that attenuate the power of positivity are:

1) An acute traumatic situation

The analyst bears the positive aspect of treatment in mind when they treat the patient in this critical situation. The psychical imbalance of the patient may require urgent measures, such as medication, an increase in the frequency of sessions, interviews with a partner or family, consultation with other professionals, or hospitalization.

2) Chronic negative therapeutic reaction

In this case, the patient´s resistance is coupled with mental apathy. Nothing is of any use, and the analyst perceives the patient's projection of powerlessness. Not only is the patient incapable of working-through, but the analyst's interpretations are dismissed. The analyst's expertise and patience come face to face with the patient's negativity and destructiveness.

3) Reaction in the face of a catastrophic total collapse of the psychical apparatus

The analyst's position is completely undermined by the impact of the *Wirklichkeit* on the patient. The analyst bears every insult with calm and composure, or deftly avoids the destructive force of the patient, like a toreador faced with a charging bull. The patient attacks the analyst, who bears the full brunt of the patient's feelings of destruction and desperation, but remains untouched. They manoeuvre slightly, just enough to keep the necessary 'trophic' distance which allows them to advance the psychoanalytic process.

Psychical consequences of working with positivity

The psychical consequences of working with positivity can be summarized as follows:

a. The forging of an alliance with the life-drive.
b. The avoidance of fixation on traumatic memories.
c. Care in avoiding the triggering of defence mechanisms.
d. Creation of a space for a psychic truce.
e. Consolidation of positivity.

f. Greater access to what is 'new', to that which has never before been experienced.
g. Facilitation of psychical change.
h. Development and intensification of positive feelings, such as joy, well-being, contentment, calm, and inner peace.
i. Lightening of the psyche.

Some remarks on technique in couple and family therapy in the light of the concept of positivity: The role of prevention

In therapeutic work with couples and the family, professionals are forced to confront the intense suffering caused by reciprocal reproaches, relational conflict, aggression, and narcissistic wounds, all of which are emotionally charged with the intensity derived from the actual presence of participants and the real life unfolding of conflictive scenarios. These are not mere fantasies: the aggressor or the loved one is present, with their burden of frustration or dissatisfaction.

In examining the vicissitudes of inter-relational treatment, I make use of the notion of *psychical distance*, which is established intersubjectively. As the analyst is steering the course of the treatment, it is their priority to ensure that this distance is respected and it is they who must transmit these limits to everyone involved, so as to build a protective screen against projections. By means of this subtle psychic veil, the dimensions of reality and fantasy are put back into perspective, and the couple or family history is rewritten without the emotional burden of characters from a past marked by neurosis.

The analyst provides an equilibrium point and functions as a psychical organizer who is able to repair the damage done by the chaos of aggressions and rejections. Their verbal and non-verbal interventions calm the disturbed psyches in order to achieve an atmosphere in which conciliation and working-through are possible.

The use of observations deriving from the reading of clinical material is another valid method in the reconstruction and understanding of what takes place in group sessions.

Patients are likely to be very sensitive to the smallest sign of disinterest on the part of the analyst or what they perceive to be the favouring of one of them over the other. The Oedipus complex, feelings of exclusion and the primal scene all play their part in the triangular relationships which might arise. The analyst may receive the approval or the criticism of the couple or of other family members.

An approach which incorporates positivity aims at a dynamic understanding of each case, the analyst's objective being to rescue that which can possibly be modified. As well as being an organizer, they are a mediator, whose task is to establish a space of non-aggression which is conducive to the generation of insights and which fosters the ability to listen. A facilitating presence, they find a way through the communicational chaos of disagreements to open up a space for working-through.

A preventative focus during treatment is of vital importance. This is mainly directed towards those members of the couple or the family who have the greatest emotional stability. The individual who is suffering and ill—I am thinking here of psychotic patients in family therapy—needs to be protected from themselves (when they manifest auto-aggressive tendencies). Furthermore, the other family members need to be protected from the damage they may suffer from this member of the family as a result of their illness.

A serious illness may contaminate the therapeutic space and give rise to pathogenic phenomena. If, during long periods, a family is constantly exposed to the illness of one of its members, and is excessively devoted to their cure, it is likely that the psychic state of one of its members may also be unhealthy. The burden of guilt, or the over-concentration of the mind in helping someone who is ill, may paradoxically be detrimental to good psychic health. The effects of this contamination may cause neurosis or psychosomatic disorders, and deprive a family of its vitality. A preventive approach involves adopting therapeutic measures aimed at deflecting the pathogenic force towards the more healthy members of the family. In preventing the spread of the death-drive, the patient and the people who surround them are simultaneously protected.

Preventative treatment requires that the professional carefully assess the patient's illness and the potential risk of this being transmitted to others, so as to take suitable measures to repair damaged relationships and to prevent the therapeutic field from exacerbating mental illness. These precautionary measures are equally important when working with families as when working with couples.

CHAPTER FOUR

Psychoanalysis and mental health

General observations

The concept of mental health contains elements that are as much universal and established as they are culture-specific. It is a 'concept in motion' and multi-determined. The expression 'in motion' suggests a certain relativity since the concept of health is modified according to the historical period, customs, prejudices and ideals.

To evaluate the state of normality of an individual, it is necessary to bear in mind social consensus regarding definitions of health and illness. Psychoanalysis, throughout the hundred years of its existence, has established certain criteria as regards good health. Some have endured over time and others have been substantially modified; Freud's theories about the psychosexuality of men and women being a case in point.

Different disciplines view the notion of health from different perspectives. I will try to demarcate psychoanalytical categories that are closely connected to the idea of mental health.

The psyche is not a static entity. It is continuously influenced by experience, the natural processes of development, life crises and the ageing process.

Good health may be the result of an ensemble of favourable psychological and environmental factors coupled with the corrections and restitution of pathogenic elements. The latter may be due to successful psychoanalytical or psychotherapeutic treatment, or to the subject's ability to learn from experience.

Nobody is completely alone. There is no life without our fellow human beings, the influence of the environment and of significant others, whether they be deeply loved or hated. The quality of interaction with the environment influences every human being at different stages of their development. One's state of health develops as a result of the influence of others and the interaction between the environment and the individual.

Factors such as positive early experiences, the good fortune of being brought up by people with sound values, and accompanying physical good health constitute a constellation of fortunate events which are predictive (but do not guarantee) mental health. In contrast, the process of living is an eminently conflictive activity, a kind of obstacle race. The better one's state of health, the greater one's ability and flexibility in overcoming the pain, problems and frustrations which are inherent in life.

Mentally sick individuals show the perverse side of their pathology in their enjoyment of suffering, which not only harms the patient but also those who surround them (*raptus neuroticus*, borderline disorders, psychotic behaviours). In contrast to the healthy 'simplicity' of a normal person, who is able to defuse the potential threat of neurotic mechanisms, is the rigidity of the mentally ill individual characterized by feelings of malaise and stereotyped answers. The dramatization of neurotic stereotypes generates a self-repeating monotonous melodrama: the same story, the same cries of complaint, the same associations.

Mental illness fluctuates between the poles of excess and monotony.

The idea that psychic well-being will be a positive side effect of the process of working-through of traumas and the resolution of symptoms possesses a grain of clinical truth, but it is incomplete. It does not take into account that the patient may become psychically infected with the suffering generated from a protracted period of treatment which has focused on the negative aspects of their illness.

The concept of psychoanalysis of mental health includes the study of the psychic consequences of the healthy aspects of the patient. Some basic assumptions for work in this area are:

1. The elimination or attenuation of pathological components.
2. The stimulation of the healthy areas of the psyche.
3. The propagation of the healthy areas of the psyche at the expense of the pathogenic ones. Good health becomes an active agent in the improvement of health.
4. Preventative work.

The healthy area of the psyche

This is presented as an entelechy, a theoretical construct which warrants further investigation. I will now look at some specific contexts which are conducive to a healthy psyche.

A) Psychic area of basic trust

This is the domain of the 'good object', conceived by Melanie Klein, even if it is small and weak in its structure. A significant other enables the process of attachment of the child and provides them with the love that is necessary for their psychic survival.

B) Conflict-free ego sphere

This is a concept developed by Hartmann (1958) in his studies on ego psychology and adaptation. This author refers to those functions which are free from conflict when he writes:

I refer to the development *outside of conflict* of perception, intention, object comprehension, thinking, language, recall-phenomena, productivity, to the well-known phases of motor development, grasping, crawling, walking and to the maturation and learning processes implicit in all these and many others (p. 23, emphasis in original).

Even though Hartmann admits that psychoanalysis, whose aim is the observation and the treatment of pathology, does not focus on these aspects of the mind, he says: *'I am not inclined, however, to underestimate the clinical importance of these functions.'*[1] A little further on he specifies:

[1] My emphasis.

I propose that we adopt the provisional term *conflict-free ego sphere* for that ensemble of functions which at any given time exert their effects outside the region of mental conflicts ... *What we don't yet have is a systematic psychoanalytic knowledge of this sphere*; we have only partial knowledge of realty fears, of defense processes in so far as they result in "normal" development ... (Hartmann, 1958, p. 12)[2].

He defines this conflict-free area as one of 'peaceful internal development'.

By describing his ideas about 'peaceful internal development', Hartmann enables us to grasp the clinical importance of this mental area, which still requires further investigation. It is related to an individual's capacity to create harmony and to achieve peace of mind.

C) Area with health-enhancing potential

The healthy area of a neurotic person or one suffering from a serious pathology can increase its potential to influence the whole of the psyche by means of adequate stimulation. This undamaged area works like a natural neutralizer of the pathogenic totality.

This notion of the stimulation of the healthy areas of the psyche has applications in the areas of prevention and health education. Creativity and liberating activities are closely connected with the functioning of the healthy area.

Psychoanalytical criteria of mental health

I will consider here some theoretical and observable clinical parameters that establish health criteria in the field of psychoanalysis.

A) Elimination or decathexis (more or less automatic) of 'useless' unpleasant representations

Unpleasant representations are useful insofar as they serve to keep painful events in mind with the aim of preventing their repetition in the future. History requires the preservation of these unpleasant memories which enfold traumatic events in a covering of pain.

What we see here is what B. Rosenberg (1991) called 'the masochism guardian of life', as opposed to the masochism of death. A positive form of masochism facilitates the retention of lucid

---

[2]My emphasis.

memories, which enables the individual to sustain an attitude of prevention against future repetition.

Enjoyment of destruction and pain occupy very small psychic areas in a healthy individual, who is able to overcome resentments with ease and without adherence to feelings of hate. They neither get easily offended nor continually dwell on sad experiences.

Unpleasant representations serve no purpose when they reach the point in which they sustain a negative rumination which feeds on itself and whose sole objective is to perpetuate the futile enjoyment of suffering. Neurosis is usually characterized by the psychic maintenance of hyper-intensive representations, which generate chronic malaise and constant suffering.

B) Swiftness of working-through

The person metabolizes and understands their personal history, working-through unpleasant moments and circumstances in order to preserve their love of life.

An inability for insight is one of the reasons for poor results in many analyses.

Thanks to the swiftness of working-through, the individual can correct false connections, overcome suffering and successfully do battle against their illness. The healthy individual is able to correct errors with ease.

C) Libido fixation on pleasant memories

Libidinal viscosity is linked to the recollection and repetition of joyful experiences.

The mind does not want to relinquish its positive memories and holds onto them tightly in a form of a pleasurable rumination. The fixation is non-traumatic and the superego observes and approves of these pleasurable thoughts. Leisure pursuits and inner spaces of freedom are experienced without feelings of guilt.

There is permission for psychic life. The ego ideal is constructed with positive expectations about the creation of joy and pleasant moments throughout life.

D) Positive destiny neurosis

Fortunate events are repeated, as if the person in question had been born under a lucky star. Whatever they do seems to produce positive results and they are thought of as 'lucky' and 'fortunate'. The life-instinct prevails.

Neurosis diminishes to allow room for positive repetition within the framework of good health and optimistic expectations of a bright future.

E) Effectiveness in actions and the taking of palliative decisions in situations of suffering

The subject is not held back by obstacles and tries to rapidly surmount them. Owing to their basic inner trust, the defence mechanisms of the ego act with flexibility in combination with the rest of the psychic agencies to protect them from an excessive invasion of harmful stimuli.

F) Good handling of minor traumatic situations

The automatic mechanisms of minimization of traumatic events allow the individual to mentally distance themselves from painful situations.

G) Narcissistic transformation (access to tertiary narcissism)

One important criterion of mental health is the ability to transform narcissism. This transformation reduces self-love and places the individual off-centre. The person gains access to tertiary narcissism (Alizade, 1995), the result of the process of transformation, which has a structuring effect. This effect has both clinical and psychosocial implications. It strengthens the individual's control over destructive impulses, and enables them to show interest in distant objects which are beyond their immediate perception. This concern for others crystallizes in a sense of solidarity.

The human being develops an awareness of the principle of relativity and accepts their fate. Egocentric narcissism, the secondary form of narcissism, restricted to the subject's self-image and to the closed circle of their loved ones, is transformed and tamed. Libido is projected onto fellow human beings.

The person becomes less vulnerable to the vicissitudes of existence as the distance between their ego and their narcissistic ideals diminishes. They are even capable of becoming good losers accepting that, in the game of life, success and failure are relative.

The narcissistic transformation towards tertiary narcissism implies a certain degree of acceptance of the finitude of life as well as a broader cosmovision of material reality.

The transformation to tertiary narcissism is a transcendent change and represents a qualitative leap. It is both a return to the grandeur of primary narcissism and implies—by means of the acquired psychic re-organization—a high level of responsibility and discernment in dealing with others. This narcissistic transformation can be observed frequently in daily life. It is not characterized by exaltation or sacrifice, which are typical of the idealization of the primary forms of narcissism. 'The tertiary form is a simple, quiet one, coexisting with a state of "being part of the world" where the principles of reality and relativity prevail. Omnipotence is contrasted with the simple inner strength of individuals who understand their limitations and the impermanence of their life. They are capable of devoting some of their energies exogamically to other human beings, who share the same condition of life and mortality in the here and now, as well as to those who will outlive them' (Alizade, 1995, p. 97).

H) The capacity to mature

In Erikson's (1997) theories on human development through their life cycle, he states that the maturity stage is characterized by caring about one's fellow man and the triad of procreativity, productivity and creativity.

These developmental stages are successfully accomplished according to the degree to which good health prevails. It is common to observe adults with infantile narcissism, children who are prematurely over-adapted, and so on. In these cases, development has come to a standstill or has missed certain phases due to underlying pathology.

I) Ethical principles

Ethical individuals cultivate healthy values as much for themselves as for the community they live in.

With the discovery of the unconscious, psychoanalysis revolutionized the concept of ethics by demonstrating that what constitutes pleasure for one psychic system is un-pleasure for another one, and by showing that we harbour hostile impulses in our unconscious which are repressed by education and culture.

The psychic agency of the superego can convert itself, on the one hand, into a guardian of responsibility and rectitude of the human being, and, on the other, into an alienating and normative structure that hinders the free expression of creativity.

J) Psychic lightness

The automatic decathexis of painful memories, the utilization of non-conflictive functions of the ego and the plasticity of defence mechanisms constitute elements that facilitate the achievement of psychic lightness.

At one end of the spectrum can be seen the heavy burden of neurosis with its concomitant feelings of guilt, libidinal fixation on negative representational-affective complexes, representational excesses, masochistic jouissance; at the other, stands the alleviation and lightness of the mind of the healthy individual, who manages to enjoy every day without unnecessarily complicating their thinking with what I term 'torturous rumination'. The insignificant, small experiences of well-being and sublimation are interwoven into the fabric of everyday life, filling the mental universe of the healthy individual and lightening their mood.

During treatment the patient gradually experiences a greater lightness as the analysis proceeds, which tends to be expressed in the form of psychic alleviation and as a state of general well-being. The functional physical symptoms related to the weight of the neurosis (muscle tension, violent headaches, dyspepsia) slowly fade.

The building of good health

The undamaged areas of the patient's psyche require very close examination. It demands careful consideration of the healthy elements of the patient's personality and the opening up of psychoanalytical listening in order to incorporate these elements into their treatment. Cathecting the patient's pleasant associations gives rise to new positive facilitations. Focusing on the undamaged part of the psyche becomes a key element in the treatment of the patient's pathology and is an important factor in helping to bring about a positive outcome.

A) Focusing on the healthy area of the psyche. Transference and good mental health

The analyst explores the healthy part of the psyche, facilitating its influence or permeation into the damaged, traumatized area.

The patient's trauma decathects owing to the increase in vital facilitations and, in many instances, an *intrapsychic de-traumatizing process* is triggered.

The analyst salvages the positive aspects of the mourning process, of the interpretation of dreams, of unresolved narcissistic and Oedipal conflicts.

In the same way that the projections of images and pathogenic conflicts generate transference neurosis, the unlocking of the patient's health potential results in the positive transference of good mental health. This is an integral part of the healing process and contributes to its positive outcome.

B) Openness of psychoanalytic listening

In general, psychoanalytical treatment is oriented towards the investigation of pathological functioning. The neurotic history of the patient contains hyper-intensive representations (Freud, 1950 [1887–1902]) which attract the attention of the analyst, who is a seasoned listener. The purpose of the treatment rests on undoing false connections and heightening the patient's awarenesss by giving them an insight into the unconscious basis of their symptoms.

Mental health does not express itself noisily. It is a backdrop that provides stability and psychic harmony. 'Peaceful internal development', as Hartmann (1958) calls it, needs to be given the chance to express itself and to gradually unfold.

The patient is listened to at an asymptomatic and non-traumatic level, observing the influence of positive psychic activity and focusing on these positive associative pathways.

It is often the case that the patient's associations are permeated with negativity. Analyst and patient are immersed in painful sessions which hold the latent promise of the resolution of complexes and the cessation of suffering by means of working-through. Using the Freudian metaphor of the surgeon, the analyst operates on the pathogenic nucleus that emanates malaise. Eventually, the patient's hopes for attaining happiness emerge on the analytical horizon. At some point along the way, the clouds clear: it is time for a psychic truce. The analyst does not let this opportunity pass and sets out to explore that which is non-traumatic with the same dedication as they have shown in exploring that which is pathological. By doing so, they stir up the patient's positive mnemic traces thus contributing to better clinical efficacy. The openness of psychoanalytical listening assigns maximum importance to pleasant, everyday *insignificancies*. It would seem that this psychological production reveals representational and affective bonds of great clinical consequence.

C) Cathexis of the healthy area of the psyche

In order to please the analyst—either because of masochistic enjoyment or their observation of the traditional analytical focus on conflictive associations—the patient may justify their 'reason for being a patient' by intensifying their manifestations of helplessness or illness. If they arrive at their sessions feeling content with their lives, they may feel that they are betraying the analytical principle of expressing their suffering. Is there sufficient justification for their being in analysis?

Realizing that the analyst is concerning him or herself with associations distant from the mental areas of conflict, the patient is surprised; this 'call to normality' provokes bewilderment.

The patient, perceiving the analyst's 'associative desire' via their questions and interpretations, includes associations related to happy memories by means of positive transference. In this way, the idealization of masochism as a narcissistic space shared with the analyst is erased. The analyst does not merely await associations that lead them to areas of crime and punishment, conflict and symptom, but rather gives libidinal weight to the non-transcendental, harmonious moments in the patient's life, to the happy, insignificant, everyday experiences that capture memory traces of satisfaction.

The observation and the awareness of positive psychic activity within the magma of psychic complexity broaden the 'defile of consciousness' (Freud, 1895d p. 294).

D) Production of new facilitations

New pathways are opened up. The flow of cathectic energy increases from these positive facilitations, whose ramifications and positive memory traces are consolidated over the course of the treatment. These facilitations have a great influence on trauma, neutralizing its pathological potential.

E) Building healthy ego-structures (Freud, 1923b)
The various elements that build better psychic health crystallize in the organization of new ego-structures[3], which combine with the results of new psychic processes generated during analysis. These structures have a protective function against life's vicissitudes.

The sensual-affective body: Health and pathology[4]

The following emphasizes the importance of the body and its physicality (carnality) for the structuring of the psyche. The positivity of a person depends closely on the quality of the sensual-affective substrate and the vicissitudes of the different stages of their life cycle. This sensual-affective foundation represents a primary matrix where—under benign conditions—the first healthy life experiences inscribe themselves upon the early psyche.

A) The sensual-affective substrate and archaic sensuality
The study of sensuality requires a detailed examination concerning the way it interconnects with instinctual and affective life. The sensual-sensorial 'proto affect' binds itself to experiences of pleasure and un-pleasure (primary affects) strengthening the sensual-affective weft.

The psychic structure has a sensual-affective basis (Alizade, 1999b), a re-edition of which takes place in the analytical field.

In the psychoanalytical setting, there are multiple body-to-body interchanges that clearly demand rules of abstinence in the physical interaction between patient and analyst: the prohibition of directly touching excludes all intimate contact: 'social relationships, aggressive acts or sexual ones' (Anzieu, 1990, p. 34). Body-to-body encounters in the analytical setting are indirect and inevitable. To a handshake or a casual greeting, which implies a direct skin-to-skin contact, we can add perceptual contact in the emission of noise, in eye contact, in olfactory interchanges, in movements. Likewise, *the*

---

[3] *Ichgestaltungen* (Freud, 1923b).

[4] This paragraph summarizes part of a text entitled 'The sensual-affective substrate and psychic structuring', presented at the 41st International Psychoanalytical Congress in Santiago de Chile in July 1999.

voice is body, which implies an act of physical participation. A voice may not always achieve the status of a word but it is able to imprint itself as an 'auditory physicality' and fulfills the function of a communicative phonic mass. It not only conveys emotions and even a variety of ideas in its scansions, silences, tones and rhythms but it also brings about transferential and counter-transferential effects: calm, anger, tedium, emotional unblocking, and the appearance of repressed ideas.

The energy generated from this indirect body-to-body contact pervades the atmosphere of the session, and is the vehicle for fantasies, wishes, resistances. Silence 'talks' and conveys messages which may be pre-verbal, mute and often profound from a domain which is beyond the word.

These primary structures which bind the analytical dyad are recreated within the context of regression, generated in the above mentioned setting. The primary sensorial psychic envelopes (rhythm, temperature, smells, sounds, voices) reappear in the analytical setting. The continuity of analysis and the frequency of the sessions facilitate the creation of a 'common skin' between the analyst and the patient (as with the primary objects in the past). The *senti* (Anzieu, 1970, pp. 806–807) or the coenesthetic universe of the protagonists of the treatment combines with verbal communication.

Sensuality, on its archaic and original level, is a sensorial-affective matrix, the site of one of the first core psychic organizers. It constitutes a sensory-perceptual complex that accompanies the developmental stages of both the individual's sensuality and their ego.

The term 'archaic sensuality' defines the primary world of sensations and perceptions, both pleasurable and un-pleasurable, this being an anchoring point for the incipient corporal ego.

An individual's sensorial awareness of their body is the precursor of the formation of the 'ego-skin' (Anzieu, 1985), which endows them with a feeling of their own individuality, and a basis for their sense of being.

The sensual body is an experiential body.

This sensorial-affective substrate requires the affects of others who, by providing this support, become a source of vital energy. Body-to-body encounters between individuals generate an interchange of psychic and physical energy: the guarantee of psychic survival.

The domain of sensuality lies beneath the stratum of affect, and close to the area of the drive: underlying and adjoining territory. The body, transversed by drives and made of organic matter, perceives and feels.

The conceptual framework of attachment theory, with its ethological perspective (Bowlby, 1989), emphasizes the role of the protective other as the guarantor of what could be termed 'psychic self-preservation'.

The marasmus of infants (Spitz, 1965) supports the theoretical hypothesis of the sensual-affective substrate as a primary organiser. If this does not exist in its positive form as a nurturing interpersonal relationship, even at a minimal level, the child will not be able to survive. Hostile feelings and indifference must occupy a secondary place. Such indifference has a devastating effect, leading to a feeling of abandonment in the infant, with fatal consequences.

This is a psychic death which takes place prior to verbal communication and is caused by the absence of the sensual-affective substrate. This substrate is generated from the life-instinct of others (external love) and provides the emotional support which sustains the psychic apparatus in its nascent state.

The life-force of fellow human beings provides the indispensable psychic sustenance for the preservation of vital functions. The incipient ego urgently needs the presence of another loving protector in order to develop a healthy 'unconditional omnipotence' (Ferenczi, 1913, p. 67).

Self-preservation underpins sexuality. The child needs care, affection, a 'word bath' (Anzieu, 1970, p. 808), a desirous interchange. Sensuality takes the form of a heterogeneous mass of physical sensations on hold, awaiting psychic survival or psychic death. Primary or archaic sensuality stems from the infant's urgent need for self-preservation.

Sensuality is also synonymous with vulnerability. At its roots, it possesses a feminizing quality, constituted by the initial pleasurable sensations of partial drives which adhere to the sensorial world. Formed from the transitivity of the child and their inevitable defencelessness, it emerges prior to the word, and belongs to the psychic world of experience. In essence pluralistic and binding, it needs the presence of another to thrive. The large mass of perceptions and sensations within the child generates motor responses which are the gateway to primary sensorial awareness.

The primitive 'pleasure-ego' (Freud, 1915c p. 136), which ejects what is unpleasant and introjects what is pleasant, interacts in intimate communion with experiences and physical sensations of satisfaction and pain. Freud writes (1915c, p. 136): 'At the very beginning, it seems, the external world, objects, and what is hated is identical.' As regards the relational structure of sensuality, that which threatens our self-preservation and our survival potential is hated. Therefore, we hate what we do not love and what does not surround and sustain us with affection and life-enhancing energy. *Helplessness hates without knowing who to hate.* It is a painful hatred, directed to the affective-sensorial void that threatens life with extinction, a hatred which still does not recognize itself as such. Hate and pain form an alliance and, after reaching a chronic state as a result of repeated frustrating experiences, attack healthy narcissism and damage mental health.

From this perspective, archaic sensuality can be redefined as a primary affect which has a place among the object complexities of adult life. It is the first instrument or mediator which establishes the infant's contact with the world. The psychophysical nakedness of the infant is rapidly covered by the sensory psychic envelopes of the environment that they are born into. These perceptual and affective psychic envelopes contain qualities which are both pleaseant and unpleasant. Primary masochism and the congenital quantum of the life-instinct or the death-instinct can be heightened or neutralized as a consequence of the effects of these initial sensorial-affective experiences on the psyche. In place of words, there is the presence of others and non-verbal sensorial-affective transmission.

Sensorial matrices and personal experiences register the first profound visceral-erogenous engrams. The body feels and these sensations are integrated within the propioceptive engrams which become interwoven with the representational universe at a later stage. The unrepresentable has primacy in the interlinking of the soma and the psyche.

The pre-word stage is fundamental in the attainment of a sense of being. It encompasses the unspeakable, the unmentionable and somatic expression. It represents the body in its pure form: sensorial, proto-affective, the place of primitive emotions.

Gradationally, we can cover the body with various layers which represent schematically a succession of different bodies: the biological body, the sensorial body, the erogenous body, the emotional body, the aesthetic body, the verbal body, the ethical body and the social body, the latter being influenced by socio-cultural norms and models (Alizade, 1992 [1999]).

In life, these different bodies unite, separate and join together in various combinations.

The function of 'sharing our bodies' (Alizade, 1992 [1999 p. 53–59]) and receiving the body of another is fundamental in life at a psychic, physical and social level. This (Alizade, 1992 [1999]) highlights the physical presence of a fellow human-being and the influence of this on psychic reality. The process of living, which involves physical interaction with others, gives bodily contact an organizing or destabilizing psychic function. It is not only important to be touched but what is also important is the context in which this touch takes place. 'Sharing our bodies with others' is a constant, daily occurrence where the life-instinct and the death-instinct both play their role. When Thanatos prevails, one's own body and the body of the other one are headed towards pain, suffering and partial destruction (sexual abuse, perversions).

Two principle positive functions stand out when body-to-body experiences take place: a) the function of obtaining pleasure (with or without jouissance), and b) the support function of the psyche (love and protection). These body-to-body experiences emerge as an adult function, which is revitalizing and protects the individual against afanisis-related anxieties and corporal disassociations.

B) Psychic maturity and positivity

In adult life, sensuality merges with erogeneity. It is a sensuality which depends on another person for its survival. The experiences of pleasure or unpleasure are not basically autoerotic: in the physical interchange with a significant other (mother, father, substitute parent, caretaker, and so on), the individual embarks on a learning process about pain and satisfaction.

Throughout the different stages of life, sensuality is interwoven into the structures that constitute the sensorial awareness of the individual: on the one hand, it is incorporated into the semantic structure and on the other, it maintains its primary function as the basis for psychic survival. The initial psychic weft gradually takes on a greater complexity and diverse experiences of pleasure and unpleasure introduce the affective element into the individual's sensorial world at an early stage.

Primogenial, archaic sensuality is re-signified during the process of growth and maturity, especially in the context of puberty, love experiences, motherhood and life crises.

Physical interaction with another person is of prime importance in physical and emotional survival. Later on, in adolescence and adulthood, satisfactory experiences deriving from the 'affective body' of another become powerful psychic stabilizers or destabilizers. Love in youth or in adult life will always be more than a mere libidinal object bond: from the depths of the psyche, experiences of love arouse memories and traumatic experiences associated with the first significant objects.

Sensuality becomes an instrument for *the objectification* and discovery of life.

The individual may often feel that they are faced with an object-choice. In reality, what is of prime importance is their need to obtain a body which has a 'nurturing' quality in the sense of a body which can provide loving and sensual experiences to trigger a sensual-affective discharge, the absence of which can lead to a state of anxiety or emotional desensitization.

By drawing attention to the theoretical importance of sensuality, it can be seen that the polarity of touching and being touched has the potential to structure or de-structure the psychic apparatus according to the benign or pernicious effect of this experience.

The pathogenesis of object relations clearly demonstrates the foundation of archaic sensuality, the analysis of which reveals the fissures and weaknesses of this sensual-affective base. Within the framework of transference, a re-edition of archaic emotions takes place. By using various approaches, the analyst endeavours to obtain the 'corrective emotional experience' (Pichon-Rivière, 1970, p. 14) that can cure the psychic damage provoked by sensual-affective insufficiency.

CHAPTER FIVE

Repetition and its reversal

Hypothesis

In this chapter I will investigate the interrelationship of repetition with different instinct categories and underlying structures.

The study of the compulsion to repeat in the service of the life-instinct constitutes a theoretic challenge. This psychic phenomenon has not been sufficiently explored in psychoanalytic theory.

In the last part of this chapter, I posit the potential detachment of the repetition compulsion from the service of the death-instinct, and the change of repetition from negative to positive (repetition for the life-instinct). This hypothesis, with respect to the reversal of repetition, challenges the idea of the immobility of the death-instinct with respect to repetition compulsion. Masochistic pleasure reaches its culmination, and the process of working-through succeeds in reverting this repetition compulsion back towards Eros.

Repetition and repetition compulsion

Repetition can be understood using a descriptive model or a genetic and explanatory model (Etchegoyen, H. 1986).

Freud (1920g) distinguished repetition from the repetition compulsion. The work of psychoanalysis has centered on the study and potential resolution of the repetition compulsion arising from the experiences of suffering.

Freud's description of repetition in 1914g as a psychic phenomenon, as a condition of remembering and forgetting, and as a way of uncovering the significant hidden events in the patient's life by means of transference, was modified in 1920g by the addition of an instinctual basis. The quality of the instinct attached to the repetitive phenomenon varies according to the interplay of forces and the stage of the patient's development. The second topography, dividing instincts into life- and death-instincts, expands the concept of repetition and emphasizes its compulsive character linked especially to the death-instinct. With this division, Beyond the Pleasure Principle opens up fascinating and sinister new territory. The human search for death in life is put in relief, with the desire to return from the state of enjoyment to the state of inertia, and the exquisite sadomasochistic tortures that take root in the psyche in a harmful fusion of drives. In sessions, the force of the death-instinct appears in negative transferential responses, in destructive actions and in the ferocity of resistances. Trauma becomes the everyday. Whatever ravaged the psyche previously is reluctant to abandon the ground it has gained.

Repetition crystallizes energy in a representational model or pattern that steers the patient towards their destiny. 'The same' that recurs is a structure manifested as a scenario where, in different guises, variations on the same scene are played out while at the same time—unbeknown to the patient themselves—it cries out for the cessation of this insistent and deadening sameness.

Repetition has been studied from different perspectives. Destiny neurosis, with its negative characteristics, passes from failure to failure. Repetitive insistence, like the rise and fall of a swell, seems to be striving for meaning again and again in its sequence and rhythm. It is like a silent voice that, in a hidden code, utters a password with the power to liberate.

Repetition and its compulsive character can be likened to a catastophe-structure, which intrudes into the individual's life with a certain aura of mystery if not magic.

The work of the negative reveals an apparently inexhaustible traumatic potential inscribed on the primary process, emanating from the depths of the unconscious, reappearing unforeseen as if by mis-chance. In the domain of 'Tyche' (Lacan, J. 1964, pp. 43–62), the real unexpectedly rears up with diabolical fury like a mythical monster from the deep. The Automaton, on the other hand, submits to repetitive boredom, to an enclosing dynamic apparently exempt from the freshness of novelty. As if there were an unavoidable, unconscious seal, the Automaton, governed by the law of signifiers, inexorably obliges the subject to occupy determinate spaces.

But that is not the end of the story. Repetition compulsion belongs to the global scope of the instincts. The life-instinct and the death-instinct coexist in different proportions according to circumstances and the mental health of the patient.

Freud (1920g) pointed out that children cannot 'have their pleasurable experiences repeated often enough' (p. 35). The pleasure that a child derives from repetition is manifest in their asking for the same story to be told over and over again. Lacan (1964), when referring to the unconscious and repetition, draws attention to the diversity inherent in repetition. The yearning for novelty underpins the tendency towards repetition. This is a novelty that is not reduced to a disguise for sameness but rather one where the psyche embarks on an exploration and conquest of a piece of previously unknown reality.

The viscosity of the libido fixes on pleasant memories as much as unpleasant ones. Once repetition is triggered, the active unconscious memory is manifested as an act (Lacan, J. 1964), be it a pleasant memory or a frustrating or traumatic one.

In the analytic session

Patients do not come to consultations because they are repeating pleasant situations. They bring a problem of persistent suffering, trauma and conflict.

Working within the repetition system constitutes a real challenge for the psychoanalyst.

Repetition hides a secret; psychoanalysis tries to unveil it. It is difficult work that touches on the 'bedrock' of the mind. It is rooted frequently in defined characteristics—'This is what I'm like; I will never change'; in the feeling of the certainty of immutability; and of the sinister.

What purpose does repetition serve? There are several possible answers:

1) To avoid knowing

Repetition has a defensive function: to keep a memory suppressed or to suppress an experience. It keeps the unnamable repressed in the depths of the psyche. The scenario that unfolds is at the same time the hiding-place of an unthinkable reality and the mysterious if not sinister manifestation of a fact costumed for dramatization.

The quality of the known stays outside the circuits of the secondary preconscious–conscious system. The hidden knowledge emerges in symptoms and appears in various illnesses depending on the pathology of the patient.

2) To search for liberation

Repetition fulfills a cathartic function. This discharge occupies centre stage. Repetition becomes a process that strives to achieve its own dissolution, a diabolical insistence driven by a vital energy. The repetition becomes compulsive and, although the pleasure of suffering appears to have primacy, the subject is fighting a hard battle to achieve their liberation.

3) To bring about mutative experience

The mutative psychic experience awakens phobic feelings and even depersonalization during the transformative process. Resistances usually hinder this profound process of change. Once these are defeated, the patient has access to new ways of thinking, achieving the psychic death of old pathogenic clichés and the birth of new representational and affective organizations. They may fear, as they sometimes express in sessions, 'returning to normal'. This fear, however, is a response to an 'other' appearing inside oneself, and to the emergence of unknown potentialities. The mutative experience is accompanied by a process of disidentification and detachment from alienating identities.

Who is this 'other' that emerges in the mind and disturbs its structure? The answer will be found by the patient him or herself, in the course of their subsequent life.

Repetition is expressed in:

a. transferential acts, gestures, and behaviours
b. rigid recollections

c. insistent and monotonous complaining
d. resistances
e. structures: Oedipal, narcissistic[1] (Marucco, N. 1996)
f. its transgenerational power
g. crisis.

In the field of analytic work, it is possible to observe two types of psychic mechanism.

a) Regression
This consists in getting close to hidden psychic knots in order to disentangle and understand them (Roudinesco, E. & Plon, M. 1997). Regressive psychic activity clashes with a sameness that is weary of itself. This weariness frequently pervades the atmosphere of the sessions when a repetition untangles itself, and the patient's despair is overwhelming, as though they were condemned to torturous monotony. Roudinesco considers that: 'This regressive psychic activity leads, by its recurrence, to the postulation of the existence of a tendency to return to our beginnings, to the state of absolute repose, the state of no-life, that which is supposed to pass for death.' This is a game of risk that is played out in the arenas of early fixations and archaic experiences.

b) Compulsion
The patient, prisoner to their repetitive state, perceives a peremptory urge that always takes them to the same place. A sinister feeling is evoked which usually accompanies the compulsion in its transition to an action. The demon from the unconscious has taken over the soul of the patient, a demon associated both with sinister psychic circularity and with the returning to sameness once more.

Reversal of repetition: From negative to positive

The driving force of repetition must be tamed so that new facilitations are made and the repetitive circuit is broken. When analytical

[1]Aslan (1993) conceptualizes it as a character structure. According to this author, we habitually work with repetitions anchored in the patient's way of perceiving, encoding and attributing meaning and not with destiny neuroses. The structural change that we try to produce in clinical work is based within the structure and not on the suppression of structural repetition, which would be impossible.

treatment is successful, it breaks the repetitive automatism and allows its reversal. This work takes place in parallel with the historization of trauma and consolidation of positivity.

The reversal of instinctual primacy—from the domain of the death-instinct to the domain of the life-instinct—is usually a gradual process when observed in neurotic and borderline patients. There is great difficulty in achieving the instinctual reversal in cases of severely traumatized psychic apparatus and when the complemental series are highly unfavourable in any of their sequences.

The instilling of immovable ideas with respect to the compulsion to repeat is an iatrogenic element present in the learning and training of this discipline. These so-called theoretical truths can drive some patients that have studied psychology or psychoanalysis to despair. It can give them a false idea that they are condemned to a life sentence having internalized a tragic instinctuality once and for all.

The reversal of repetition manifests itself in a variety of ways. Its complexity requires that not just the plurality of theorizations about instincts be considered, but also the structural mental framework in which they interact. The more the automaton adheres to the death-instinct that dominates the psychic life of the patient, the greater the analytical challenge.

In the analytical work, small clinical signs indicate that the process of reversal of repetition is in motion. Some of the necessary conditions in this transition are:

1) Dismissal of the idea of unchangeable destiny: the role of the conscious

The patient not only struggles against unconscious resistances but also consciously faces despair and the mistaken certainty that repetition is supreme in their pathology. Fundamental in changing this belief is the work of the conscious and the will of the patient, together with their confidence in the scope and benefits of their treatment as it progresses.

Freud wrote a paper about the meta-psychology of the conscious and then destroyed it. It is clear that he did not find it simple to reconcile the role of the conscious with the psychoanalytic adventure.

The collaboration of the patient in the business of analysis includes the participation of their conscious desire to struggle against the demons of their unconscious, to conquer their resistances and to halt the acting-out which stems from these resistances. The conscious and the unconscious mutually interact.

The resisting patient may take refuge in the pretext that their unconscious is supreme in its pathogenic power. Rationalization, based on theoretical clichés, protects the unconscious from the force of the conscious will of the patient. In a kind of psychic laziness, they surrender themselves to the couch and wait for the analyst to do all the work. Every so often, discouraged and despondent, they criticize the analyst's lack of ability in producing the desired outcome.

2) Working-through and intelligence

Although working-through is a phenomenon eminently unconscious–preconscious, the process of working-through requires that the conscious of the patient is both focused and persevering, that it accepts the analytic challenge and allies itself with the mind of the analyst in their strong desire for a successful outcome. It is probable that the capacity for successful working-through is closely related to intelligence. The contribution of intelligence to the effort of working-through allows the disentangling of false connections and the achievement of adequate disidentifications.

This may explain the poor results of the treatment of neurotic patients, although this notion requires further investigation.

3) Daring

The patient increases their desire for knowledge in the process of analysis and dares, by way of the presence of the analyst, to explore 'even further' their inner world. They are not thwarted by obstacles and, in spite of resistances and fears, continue the process of analysis. Freud (1914g) wrote: 'He must find the courage to direct his attention to the phenomena of his illness. His illness itself must no longer seem to him contemptible, but must become an enemy worthy of his mettle, a piece of his personality, which has solid ground for its existence and out of which things of value for his future life have to be derived' (p. 152).

4) Receptiveness to the learning process

Etchegoyen (1986) quotes Lagache who introduces the idea of habit to account for transferential repetition. Based on the theory of the learning process, he states that it would seem that positive transference utilizes habits that permit learning while negative transference impedes the learning process.

The patient absorbs the knowledge of the art of living that the analyst procures. As a result, the analyst acquires enormous importance over the course of the treatment. The analyst offers him or herself to be an object for projections of the patient's life history. Their function is more important still by virtue of their inevitably becoming an identificatory model and educator.

I will now present some situations and indications that, from the clinical perspective, signal the reversal of repetition.

1) The proximity of the catastrophe point (Thom, R. 1980)

Catastrophe opens the repetitive system to a new order of experiences. Arriving at the catastrophe point, the psyche dares to launch itself into the unknown. At this point, the repetitive avatar culminates and a *different series* is started. Patience and tolerance are required in order to detect, inside the appearance of sameness, the tiny newness that is waiting to have the psychic opportunity to make itself heard.

The experience of the proximity of the catastrophe point can increase the defense mechanisms of avoidance (phobia of the nearness of transformation), as explained previously. Sometimes this coexists with a certain aggravation during the treatment. Although the symptomatic turmoil can worry the analyst, it is pertinent to evoke the famous phrase attributed to Don Quixote: 'When they bark, it means we're on our way.'

The rhythmical swell of repetition returns time and again to its start point. The sessions are filled with intense experiences. Crossing the point of origin of repetition is a major experience in the analytic process. This can be likened to a journey from death to resurrection. A different life history will now have the opportunity to be written.

2) The diminishing of the viscosity of the libido

Using an image, it is valid to say that the libido passes from a viscous to a liquid state. Regression goes in search of repressed memories, dreams and screen memories. The increased potential to associate clearly shows the freedom of the libido. Curiosity about 'oneself' unfolds amid expressions of sadness and hate. The points of fixation become detached from the libido.

3) De-dramatization of the narrative

The level of dramatization in the patient's discourse decreases. Symbolic representations forge new pathways. The analyst acts as a facilitating agent, opening the door to new associations and suggesting new affective-representational models. Identification of the patient with these vital aspects of the analyst becomes an instrument of change.

4) Change in the affective tone of the session

Within the atmosphere of suffering, periods occur in which the psychic atmosphere lightens. This change produces feelings of calm and well-being.

Some sessions take place where the associative material is non-pathogenic, in which positive experiences are recalled. Pleasant feelings emerge. Laughter and happiness make their presence felt.

Two theoretic and technical correlations are:

1) The taming of the death-instinct

Freud (1937c) wittily drew on a Witch Metapsychology when he had to comment on the psychic mechanisms which are required to achieve the taming of the instincts. The masochistic compulsion to repeat is offset by the continuity of interpretative and elaborative work session after session, working towards the defeat of psychic death and the liberation of psychic life. Facilitations of psychic death lose force as new, positive facilitations proliferate where the possibility of a new destiny comes into play.

2) Refocusing the patient's associations

Like dreams, repetition permits the reconstruction of the life history of the patient and is useful even in the darkest depths of a negative therapeutic reaction. This is a well-trodden path in analysis. Repetitive insistence indicates the desire to regress, the purpose being the annihilation of this scenario, where the same returns in various guises. Monotony conceals the desire for the new.

Technically, it can prove to be effective if the analyst does not respond to the blind movements of repetition, understood to be a defence mechanism. This strategy enables the focus of the treatment to shift so that repetition no longer takes centre-stage. The analyst moves away from this persistent, central focus and explores the surrounding psychic territory with the aim of deactivating the patient's resistances.

CHAPTER SIX

Trauma and positivity

Preliminary considerations

Each patient comes to the analytical session with their own burden of suffering. They come to tell us about what is not going well in their lives in search of relief from the pain of their disturbed psyche.

The external world can easily be transformed into a source of trauma due to both the increase in aggressive stimuli from the media and the extreme narcissization of a Western individualist social system.

Our support structures (family, school, official institutions) no longer provide us with the same sense of protection. Social traumas, resulting from a variety of sources of terror, have repercussions for future generations. Our children's infancies are haunted by past echoes of war and destruction. The parent who has lived through a war wrecks their child's ability to enjoy life, while another who has endured hunger becomes a miser tormented by money and in the process transfers their own unhappiness onto their offspring. The complemental series (Freud, S. 1916–1917) appears to have a tendency to lean towards the destructive.

A variety of traumas exist and not all inhabit the same psychic space. There are major and minor traumas and, furthermore, the resulting impact of a trauma on a healthy mind is not the same as that on one which is unhealthy.

Trauma can be constructive, acting as a mental organizer, or be disruptive and disorganizing. The plasticity of the ego, the capacity to underestimate the potential traumatic impact of a situation, the forming of the trauma by means of wrapping oneself in protective anguish are all elements that protect against the pathogenic force of a specific harmful stimulus.

Baranger and Mom (1988) described different axes which underpin the problematic factors of trauma: the death-instinct, aetiology, the *a posteriori*, repetition and temporality. They state that: 'Thus, we have disorganizing, invading and paralyzing traumas, and at the opposite end of the spectrum, traumas constructed in an open temporal historicization. In the middle, we find more or less failed attempts to bind the thanatic invasion with repetition' (p. 123).

As a consequence, certain questions arise: Which psychic mechanisms are instrumental in the resolution of trauma? What happens when a trauma has certain qualities that render it impossible to be worked through? What are the factors which dictate whether one person will cope better or worse than another with a traumatic experience? Is it always necessary to historicize a trauma?

I shall attempt to find the answers to these incipient questions in the pages which follow. Initially, I will delimit the terminology related to trauma before considering the theory of technique and how it relates to positivity.

Effects

I will now detail the effects of the changes which a stimulus can have on the psyche. The list of effects is extensive and their definitions, broad. I shall mention the most important effects in terms of psychic consequences and will also include those with the potential to cause harm, which can be defined as trauma at a later stage of the patient's analysis.

Some effects, owing to their subliminal nature, go unnoticed by the conscious and must reach a higher threshold to be consciously perceived. At that moment, a sensation of discovery or surprise occurs before that which is obvious but has nonetheless remained largely ignored. This discovery takes the effect out of the realm of the subliminal and converts it into an experience. The accompanying affective tonality spans the extensive affective range which extends from pleasure to unpleasure.

A) Organizing and disorganizing effects of the affects of others in the early psyche

The affects 'of others' are to a large extent our own. The bodies of the child and mother coexist in tight communion in a type of unique, shared body. In the moments following childbirth, the sustaining body of the mother is at one and the same time both separate from and part of the infans. The physical life received from the mother, by means of the placenta, is re-edited in the world at a psycho-physical level. The mass of primary experience and the organic, sentient, perceptive mass of the newborn, immersed in experiences of satisfaction and pain, is vulnerable to the affects originating from this other, known as mother, or primary object, or that object who provides life outside of the uterus. This fellow human being, of an intimate and loving nature, occupies a vital role as guarantor of survival. The consolidation of basic trust, of the good internal object, depends to a great extent on these initial human interactions in which love can be equated to the providing of nourishment. This elementary psychic nutrition or psychic nourishment (Alizade, A.M. 1999b) plays a fundamental role in the earliest moments of existence.

B) Organizing and disorganizing effects in the understanding of reality

From the very start, the inner world of the infans favours the distortion of outside reality. The primitive 'reality ego', which can distinguish between the external and the internal, is soon replaced by the purified 'pleasure-ego' (Freud, S. 1915c). Although short-lived, the incipient perception between the outside and the inside is discussed by Freud in his work on the hypothetical initial stage of the ego. Once the primitive 'reality-ego' is discarded, the 'pleasure-ego' unifies that which belongs to others, that which is hated and that which is external. In principle, they are identical and as such we have the following basic principle: primary effects distort our perception of reality. From which originates the Freudian concept of psychic reality.

This psychic reality, or *Realität* in German, highlights our way of understanding reality within the framework of our fantasies and deceptive discourse. Life experiences and the work of analysis reduce the distortion inherent in conflicts and mental illnesses. This includes fragments of material truth which had previously remained ignored. This material truth, or *Wirklichkeit*, is only partially understandable.

We are restricted to experiencing a previously determined and limited sensory spectrum: colours, distances, sounds, rhythms and so forth. There exists an enormous realm beyond our perceptions that we can only learn to understand artificially, by means of our intellect and which is subject to our mental self-defence mechanisms in the face of the shocking and unimaginable *Wirklichkeit* of the expanding universe (Cardozo de Suarez, E., Rusconi, J. & y Bondorevsky, M. 1983).

The real (Faladé, S. 1974) is what is, the day and the night and so forth. Reality ties the imaginary to the symbolic and the real is there from the very beginning. It is both what exists in a perceivable form and in a register which is impossible to grasp. This impossibility is challenged time and time again as layer upon layer of experience of the real are continuously interwoven into the psyche, in a manner which is always insufficient. The poet T.S. Eliot wrote (1935): 'Go, go, go said the bird: human kind/Cannot bear very much reality'.

Various psychoanalysts (Puget, J., de Bianchedi, E.T., Bianchedi, M., Braun, J. & Pelento, M. 1993) have explored the concept of social reality to create an order of reality based upon the relationship between the ego of an individual and other fellow human beings. They coined the term 'transubjectivity' to take account of the phenomenon inherent in this aspect of reality.

C) Organizing and maturative effects of primal fantasies

Frustration is an effect, or microtrauma, necessary for the organization and maturing of the mind. Obstacles, prohibition and the authority established by the male hierarchy are other such organizing components in the development of a child.

The microtrauma of frustration is closely linked to the intrapsychic dynamic arising from primal fantasies whose phylogenetic origin was suggested by Freud (1915f p. 269). They lay the foundations upon which the traumatic condition lies: 1) seduction; 2) castration;

3) primal scene; and 4) intrauterine life. These complex structures of representations constitute the nuclei of attraction in the structuring of thought. The first three fantasies are linked primarily to the principle of unpleasure (seduction as a prelude to subsequent abandonment; castration as the root of existential anxiety; and the primal scene as a source of suffering in the face of exclusion). Only the desire to return to intrauterine life, anchored firmly in the principle of nirvana, promises relief when faced with the harsh reality of life. As is indicated by Laplanche and Pontalis (1968), our origins are represented by these scenes: sexual origin in seduction; the origin of the difference between the sexes in castration; the origin of the subject in the primal scene; and lastly, the origin of life in the fantasy of intrauterine life.

The importance and relevance of these fantasies support my hypothesis of a *minimum universal trauma* which is inevitably and unavoidably linked to the mortal human condition: birth, existence, struggle, passage and death. This trauma is metabolized in different ways and there exist numerous defence mechanisms to protect against this perception which, in many cases, verge on the intolerable.

Traumas and their names: Partial classification

All Freud's commentators agree that the concept of psychic trauma evolves considerably as Freud elaborates, and modifies the theoretical edifice of psychoanalysis; they also agree on the meaning of this evolution: progressive broadening of the connotation of the concept; a growing movement away from the medical concept of trauma as a brusque breaking in on organic homeostasis or as injury; increasing diversity and complexity of traumatic situations; more complex psychology (Baranger, M., Baranger, W. & Mom, J.M. 1988).

It is difficult to pin down trauma to a universally understood and accepted notion. A possible definition of trauma is that it is an influx of stimuli of such intensity that invasive, destructive effects are produced on the psyche.

I will attempt to establish an empirical classification of traumatic phenomena. What I will endeavour to highlight particularly are the different forms of clinical work within the sphere of trauma which can help to unbind it from its pathogenic and *contaminating* context.

At the same time I will seek to focus on positivity as a peripheral or separate area of work whose effects should be evaluated, investigated and developed. I will also include the concepts of *positive accumulation* and of *positive trauma* with the aim of showing the beneficial, accumulative effects.

I will list different types of traumas and will describe their specific characteristics.

A) Universal trauma, basic narcissistic trauma and trauma of 'the future'
Universal trauma or trauma of 'the future' are traumas which are an integral part of the psychic apparatus and are engrained in the human condition. Their precursor is the trauma of birth, understood to be an enormous influx of stimuli which suddenly invade the incipient being. This trauma is a natural and inevitable requisite to begin life and possesses a non-traumatic organizing character in that it fulfills an adaptive function. At the other end of the spectrum is the trauma of impermanence and transience, which could also be referred to as the trauma of death. It is a potential trauma, of the future, with many psychic consequences.

The traumatic matrix triggers conflicts and brings our defence mechanisms into play. Some contribute to the maturation of the human being as well as the elaboration of narcissism. In contrast, others lead to greater immaturity and unbounded self-love (Freud, S. 1919h) with the objective of alleviating anxieties about death and of disavowing reality.

The newborn's feeling of helplessness represents the small universal drama of the defencelessness of all living beings. The instinct to master and the problems that accompany power, relieve this feeling of helplessness. Omnipotence and narcissistic pathologies have a common root: to enjoy an illusion of immortality based on domination and submission and to exorcize the reality of insignificance. Universal trauma contains fantasmatic, biological and existentialist elements.

The fantasmic has many different strands. Narcissistic ideals and the powerful, immortal unconscious generate narcissistic pathologies (senile megalomanias, depressions, paranoias) and the mid-life crisis. In some cases, these pathologies owe their intensity to the complete inability to accept the pain of the mourning for the loss of our own life. Defence mechanisms and many hypomanic acting-outs tend to ignore the evidence provided by the nature of finitude. Our inexorable death forces the psyche into a type of conflict anticipated by the loss of life (Alizade, A.M. 2000).

The biological aspect is represented by ageing and the physical deterioration of the body to a greater or lesser extent. Faced with the signs of our own mortality, (Alizade, A.M. 1995) we silently bemoan the short time that we walk the earth. Everything that exists will ultimately stop existing and will be transformed in its passage back to the non-physical.

Baranger, Baranger and Mom (1988) highlight a trauma that is present in the first complemental series: the trauma of pre-historic experiences (the great trauma of the murder of the father and of castration). This is hereditary, ancestral trauma, experienced in a bygone era of humanity. It can be distinguished from the universal trauma of the human species in that it is a historic trauma and is part of a millennial legend.

The trauma of 'that which is to come' is not related to the death of the father, nor indeed to the death of the phallus, but rather to one's own death, that death which cannot be represented in terms of the real, and which is fantasized about and symbolized in many forms. It is a trauma that we become increasingly aware of as we go through life and gradually come to terms with our own mortality, each of us at our own psychic pace.

B) Positive trauma and positive accumulation

The word *trauma* is used in this context to mean when the psyche receives an excess of stimuli or excessive excitation which, although seemingly beneficial, can become dangerous owing to multiple factors such as the difficulty in metabolizing the sheer volume of such stimuli, unconscious feelings of guilt, envy projected onto oneself and so on.

A *positive accumulation* takes place as the first step prior to the advent of the traumatic situation. I introduce here the category of positive accumulation to indicate the build-up of vital stimuli in an individual in a short space of time. This build-up is often accompanied by a feeling of well-being and happiness when the subject manages to accept the rewards that life can bring.

If the influx of positive stimuli is too great and the individual's psychoneurosis does not permit this positive experience, then positive accumulation can destabilize the psyche: confusion, surprise, a feeling of incredulity in the face of such good fortune, an experience of depersonalization, constitute just some of its possible manifestations.

If the positive accumulation of stimuli is not processed in a healthy manner, it can be categorized as trauma. The person who is 'positivized' by a sequence of favourable events must face the psychic consequences resulting from the feeling of an 'overload' of well-being.

The individual's previous state of health will provide an indication as to which route this positive accumulation will take.

The external manifestation of the event may be positive but internally the psyche suffers from the impact of such an unexpected event. This phenomenon is related to this event being a genuine and unexpected stroke of luck.

Owing to the unpredictability and the impact of this good fortune, it is transformed into a setback which demands a change in both the individual's world view and their lifestyle. The psychic apparatus is impelled into a process of elaboration, the reversal of repetition, for which it is unprepared. It is an unevenly matched fight: external success disturbs libidinal economy and the meta-psychological organizing structures reel from the shockwave.

The demons of the inner world rise up. As mentioned previously, the unconscious feelings of guilt, the effects of the envy of others turned inwards against oneself, the punishment of the superego and masochism are just some of the internal components which conspire against the fortuitous event. The comedy threatens to descend into tragedy.

A simple example is that of the masochistic personality who receives undeniable evidence from the outside world of their value and self-esteem. Such an individual, with this negative facilitation, will attempt to divert the favourable course of destiny with the aim of securing its failure, a consequence of which being the ensuing eroticization of suffering.

Another common example is the case of the person who wins a substantial amount of money gambling only to have a fatal accident shortly afterwards.

C) Infantile sexual trauma

A memory or event from childhood can be elevated to the order of trauma, acquiring a traumatic character. The passing of time lends new meaning to a scene from the past. The repressed returns as a symptom. The memory causes suffering as it invades the psyche, and takes root in the unconscious. Traumas continue to surface during the analytical process and in the analytical field they are heard, worked through and, with luck, buried for good. Freud wrote in-depth about the psychic consequences of childhood traumas.

D) Residual organizing trauma (Blos, P. 1979)

This trauma is shaped by the residue of the inevitable harmful experiences that took place during infancy. Blos (1979) states that: 'There remains, nevertheless, at the end of adolescence a residue that challenges the adaptive resourcefulness of the late adolescent. Idiosyncratic vulnerabilities due to residual trauma are part of the human condition' (p. 417).

This type of trauma cannot be resolved and acts as a key element in the engine of socialization of the adolescent on their path to adulthood. As a means of coping with traumatic residues, the adolescent leaves the 'child' behind and embarks on the adult quest for work and involvement in different social groups.

In essence the residual trauma serves as an organizer that promotes the consolidation of the adult personality and accounts for its uniqueness. The socialization of residual trauma is heralded in therapy whenever the young patient takes over the responsibility for his own life (p. 418).

In this theoretical conceptualization of trauma, the idea of the inevitability and even the necessity of crossing traumatic barriers in the developmental process is seen once more. From this perspective, trauma acquires a positive connotation, giving structure to the psyche.

E) Classic trauma caused by a specific event (Baranger, M., Baranger, W. & Mom, J.M. 1988)

This is the trauma of the classic traumatic neurosis when a psychic catastrophe occurs (sudden illness, an accident, unexpected conflict, war neurosis). The repetition of dreams connected to war or an accident reveal the compulsion towards repetition, the tendency to elaborate and the awakening of the death-drive.

F) Pure trauma

This form of trauma was conceptualized by Baranger and Mom (1988) and is also known as empty trauma. Requiring immediate historization, it occurs when the psychic spaces it inhabits consist solely of huge reservoirs of the death-drive.

G) State trauma

The State, understood to be the ruling government in a given social milieu is, in theory, principally concerned with the well-being of its citizens. The State's failure to protect its citizens turns into a risk factor at both a physical and mental level.

This trauma can become manifest or remain latent depending on the degree to which social discontent is externalized. It can be the effect of simple cultural malaise or of genuine trauma. In the case of the latter, catastrophic feelings abound while fantasies of exile or anguish-inducing uncertainty also emerge. In those cases in which an individual has converted their narcissism into tertiary narcissism (Alizade, M.A. 1995) a sense of solidarity is felt towards distant objects who are suffering the effects of a life where they are constantly in a state of helplessness and at risk.

Some traumatic social factors induced by the State include unemployment, a high crime rate, injustice and corruption. These in turn generate desperation, anguish, and aggression against the media, palliative addictions (alcoholism amongst others) and various other psychosomatic conditions.

Freud (1940a [1938]) examines the formation of the superego and emphasizes the internalization of public opinion within it, and the influence of educators, making it the internal representative of the real external world and the direct voice of the aspirations of the ego. He writes: 'This parental influence of course includes in its operation not only the personalities of the actual parents but also the family, racial and national traditions handed on through them, as well as the demands of the immediate social milieu which they represent' (p. 146).

As the real outside world corrupts ethical principles, it contributes to the formation of corrupt ideals in future generations. The superego loses its function as the guardian of a moral conscience that aspires towards community-based ideals. Ethics are put on hold.

Negativity, in the sense of a destructive influence on the community, filters down from government powers before settling insidiously in the minds of the citizens. The parental-social example spreads and manages, in many cases, to dangerously become internalized in the superego of adults, contaminated by 'psychic rubbish' and inoculated with the bad example set by the authorities and the mechanisms of social control. These destructive deviations are passed on to future generations through a style of education that is based on anti-ethics and perversity.

H) Traumatization by the media

This is an *indirect traumatization*, manifest or latent, with enormous social repercussions. External elements, produced by technology, invade the human community. Garma, A., Allegro, L., de Arbiser, S., Arbiser, A., de Ferrer S., Garma E., Salas E., Schlossberg T., Weissman F., Winocur J. (1978) highlight the continual disintegration of the family as a result of the influence of the media which interferes with the perception of reality. They write: 'Technology imposes on us a perceived reality that goes beyond our biological ability to perceive things.' They place great emphasis upon the ability to distort reality stemming from the enormous quantity and the distorted nature of information.

Children and adolescents learn violence from television. This passive, visual learning is internalized in a mimetic identification with evil anti-heroes. The violence manifests itself at a later date and is directed towards real people with the result that society today includes children who attack, adolescent criminals and so forth.

Urban warfare has spread across our cities. State violence (the violence of corruption, of indifference towards fellow citizens and so on) forms an alliance with this other brand of violence that has been learned from the school of the small-screen that is television, and is vented on society ... resulting in yet more violence. Television replaces reflective thought (Sahovaler, J. 1997).

Karl Popper (1992) is very clear when he writes that television corrupts humanity. He attributes to this means of communication an enormous influence in both inciting crime as a way of exalting human values. He recommends that it be strictly controlled in order to protect future generations from its destructive influences.

I) The trauma of horror

Excessive traumatization (Gubrich-Simitis, I. 1979) is the invasion of the psyche and of the body by highly disorganized and destructive stimuli (torture, wars).

If the person survives such traumatization, they will have to endure the harmful after-effects of the ordeal that they have suffered. The abreactive and elaborative function of therapy directly following the event is crucial. Remaining silent and keeping the horror within are contraindicative attitudes that can inflict chronic psychic damage (Perren-Klingler, G. 1996). According to Perren-Klingler, group work with people who have undergone similar experiences is vitally important. The individual must realize that what they are experiencing does not constitute a mental illness but is rather a normal consequence of what they have suffered. He describes group therapy sessions in which the individual works through this trauma by means of recounting their experience before a group audience, describing the traumatic situation step-by-step with the greatest possible objectivity, as if it was a story being told from the outside, devoid of all emotion. The objective is to disassociate the cognitive from the emotional and to place the event in its cultural, political and social context. A great deal of time is required, both externally and internally, to allow the mind to recover and to be able to re-establish a satisfactory connection with life; residual symptoms will always remain, as will inerasable psychic scars.

A multiplicity of factors combines to influence the evolution and resolution of these traumatic events. When psychic circumstances are adverse, life is weighed down as if by the heavy burden of condemnation until the individual is liberated of their suffering by means of the onset of a serious illness or an act of self-annihilation. The mind tries to free itself of trauma at any cost, the healthy part finding itself no longer capable of tolerating the persistence of, or coexistence with, the damaged area. Traumatic memories act as a type of internal 'maddening object' (Garcia Badaracco, J. 1985, p. 133–146) whose neutralization is not always possible.

According to S. Amati-Sas[1], the person who lives through an excessive traumatic experience acquires experiential knowledge into the predatory-destructive potential of humanity which alters their entire world view forever.

It is my opinion that the positive, in terms of a therapeutic strategy, consists in the possibility of sharing with others these experiences of horror. The analyst supports the patient within a protective

[1] 1999. Personal communication.

shield of containment. What takes place is a sharing of knowledge about the danger of, existence of, and potential for, evil, a sharing which lasts forever. The voice of these experiences emanates from the flesh and blood of an individual who has lived through a trauma and this in turn modifies the psyche. It is not merely a case of mourning and trying to close wounds, it is about acquiring a fundamental and transforming insight into social enmity.

I have compared it to the experiential knowledge of the near death of many people who have lived through life-threatening experiences and who later work through this trauma, coming to terms with their own mortality. In these cases, it is necessary to dissolve the barrier between both the individual who did not personally live through the horror and the individual who did, or between the person who is still alive and the one who is about to die.

Freud (1919d) makes a distinction between the ego of peace and the warrior ego of the soldier. He states that: 'The theory of the sexual aetiology of the neurosis, or, as we prefer to say, the libido theory of the neurosis, was originally put forward only in relation to the transference neurosis of peace time' (p. 209). In this short text, he enters into the territory of war neurosis, threatening the universal sexual aetiology of neurosis. He seeks to unify external and internal danger. The unifying concept that he postulates leads him to suggest the existence of an elementary traumatic neurosis. He writes: 'The theoretical difficulties standing in the way of a unifying hypothesis of this kind do not seem insuperable: after all, we have a perfect right to describe repression, which lies at the basis of every neurosis, as a reaction to trauma—as an elementary traumatic neurosis' (p. 210).

Clinical work shows that, in spite of the complexity of overdetermination and the symptomatic multicausality of traumas, child sexual traumas differ qualitatively and quantitatively from the catastrophic traumas of horror. The latter, in some cases, produces a type of irreversible dismantling of the psyche as well as an everlasting basic distrust towards all human beings. The elementary traumatic neurosis receives a massive accumulation of destructive stimuli as the pain of the flesh (torture) combines with the pain of the psyche (in the face of evil).

It may be the case that mercenaries do not suffer from the nightmares and pathologies caused by the horrors of war. Exhaustive interdisciplinary research would improve our understanding of the complexity of this mental perversion.

I would like to quote J. Kristeva in response to a paper that we sent her (Alizade, A.M., Aptekman, M., Gerst, W., Siedmann de Armesto, M., Weissmann, F. and Weissmann, J.C. 1993) when she writes:

> Historical horror mobilises counter transference and makes patients who have been victims difficult to analyse. Unless, perhaps, the abjectness of the trauma is revived in the treatment, allowing it to be interpreted. But how many of us could stand this perversion, albeit microcosmic in scale, and could distance ourselves from it? If the psychoanalyst should need to reject this experience, I fear that they might also have to renounce their historic role (cited in Alizade, A.M. 1995, p. 92).

The sublimation of the death-drive, thought not yet completely unravelled meta-psychologically, can constitute a life-line in the recovery of severely traumatized people.[2]

Working with such people is a privilege experienced by few analysts. It is indeed a secret privilege, a paradoxical luxury in that it requires working with psychic hell.

Retraumatizing iatrogenesis

Retraumatization occurs when there is a repeated reactivation at some time of the pathogenic material which had previously been impossible to work through. This leads to the emergence of an iatrogenic circuit. The futile reworking of trauma, with the addition of some details

[2] I would like to cite a paragraph of Rosolato, G. (1989, p. 38). He writes: 'Nowadays, with atomic energy, the powers of destruction have an instrument which can bring about an absolute end, total death, both for others and for oneself'; thus the reflections of P.J. Jouve, in his preface to Sueur de Sang (1935), written in 1933 and entitled 'The unconscious, spirituality and catastrophe', have great prophetic value. By chance, I read this a short while ago. He hoped, above all, that sublimation could defeat that which still remained nameless, that is the catastrophe of civilization prey to the death-drive, whose sole concern is, 'pure destruction, and the search for a guilty party who is the object of hatred and of regression'. We now know that this 'miracle' can only come about when there is equilibrium between Eros and Thanatos, and from the 'energetic' transmutations of our desires. This also involves sublimation not just of sex but also of death, the product of violence, thanks to which love, which for P.J. Jouve finds 'an inner vehicle' in poetry, triumphs.

or even an innovative interpretation, has no effect. The analyst has reached a point of unanalysability (the process of working-through has come to a standstill) with regard to this complex.

It is pointless to keep trying with the analysis. This only results in reactivating time and time again the same mnemic traces, fixing the traumatic associative connections and creating an ever greater attachment between the patient and their traumatic experiences. A depressing monotony pervades the duration of the sessions. A form of neuronal over-learning, which is both retraumatizing and iatrogenic, sets in. Whilst it is possible that the patient will still submit to the authority of the analyst, their resistance to change and insurmountable defence mechanisms will render analysis ineffective.

The sessions continue until no further possible analysis can take place and one of the analytical dyad decides to withdraw.

In the light of what has been said above, those who arrive at the psychoanalytical sessions suffering from the effects of a traumatic experience must be treated and evaluated with great care and caution. This is due to the fact that, over the course of countless sessions, their associative pathways have been overworked and drained of any value due to the activation of a nucleus which was unhealthy or illness-inducing.

This network of associative pathways, instead of opening the way to new territory, covers the same ground without making any new associative, liberating connection. What the analyst is dealing with is the pseudo-networking of associative pathways.

There exists the risk of immersing the patient in a *new trauma created by the constant revival of memories of the old trauma* and of increasing the secondary benefit of the illness by encouraging the patient to take the role of the victim. This chronic retraumatization intensifies masochistic fixations as well as negative hyper-association inside the same network of representations.

The energy consumed by the traumatic complex absorbs the individual's life-force and the associative-interpretive repetition which takes place overruns the time limit, set according to the analyst's skill and judgement, exacerbating and strengthening the pathology.

Repeated questioning or the offering of interpretations only serves to fix the patient's masochistic tendencies.

The patient-analyst alliance can also be iatrogenic when both conclude that the former's grief and suffering is of such enormity that it is irreducible. A destructive alliance or complicity is produced which stimulates the death-instinct with its potential for annihilation. It is at this point that the analyst's own ideology comes into play: their personal reading of clinical material and ideas regarding the value of pain as an instrument capable of providing liberation from a greater suffering. Excessive expression of commiseration for the misfortune suffered by the patient tends to hide feelings of repressed hostility (false compassion) and feelings of failure in the face of defeat in the analytical battle.

In cases of excessive traumatization, the counter-transference of the analyst does not succeed in preventing feelings of indignation.[3]

In all cases, *I consider the presence of hope to be an obligation.* This demands a utopic framework and a certain humility when looking to the future. The patient has the right to *transform their suffering into a source of learning*. The cultivation of hate and the failure to develop the sublimatory mechanisms deprive the patient of their vitality and the potential for transformation.

In operational terms, the analyst splits their mind to salvage the undamaged areas of the psyche to strengthen them in an attempt to improve the health of the patient. The gradual fading of feelings of hatred and resentment allow the re-establishment of connections between the subject and their life-instinct. This stage is crucial in the prevention of illnesses resulting from stress and chronic depression. Hatred which is resistant to working through and feelings of resentment 'towards death' sap enormous reserves of libidinal energy. They prevent the carrying out and completion of key life-projects and result in pathology. The suffering subject becomes accustomed to tirelessly *torturing their torture*.

Clinical objectives

a) Forgetting and farewell: the psychoanalysis of forgetting

The process of working through and the revival of memories are aimed at erasing the traumatic complex so that the patient arrives at a psychic 'enough is enough', where they decisively cut all ties with their harrowing past. The psychic burden lightens and the psychic

[3] Amati-Sas, S. (1999). Personal communication.

apparatus finds representational and affective calm. The patient remembers to the point of forgetting, giving to those traumatic scenes sufficient meaning to guard against an excess of emotions. The memory decathects the traumatic memory traces and becomes free to explore new cathectic pathways which are linked to the life-instinct.

This type of *psychoanalysis of forgetting* demands the cessation of repetitive mental rumination and requires psychoanalytical exploration of masochistic pleasure and the *phobia of the new (phobia of life)*. Familiarization with the pathogenic mental state and being in permanent contact with unhealthy complexes require the process of mourning, this being inherent in the process of forgetting. The patient must summon up their reserves of courage to deal with the temporary trophic void once their conflicting representations and affects disappear.

b) Acceptable coexistence with trauma

There are some memories and internal configurations which remain impossible to forget or decathect. The therapeutic objective lies in seeking to tame the trauma. Trauma once tamed, becomes integrated into the functioning of the psychic apparatus. This requires that mechanisms such as the acceptance of destiny, repression and the capacity for operative disassociation are brought into play.

c) Trophic encapsulation

Trophic encapsulation utilizes the mechanism of silence. The trauma is dormant and stirs in the preconscious. It can only be shared at special moments and with specific people. This traumatic resolution is observed in people suffering from major traumas.

As Jack Fuchs (Alizade, A.M., Aptekman, M., Gerst, W., Siedmann de Armesto, M., Weissmann, F. & Weissman, J.C. 1993, p. 776) said:

> When I give a testimony, children ask me very direct questions, not like adults ... What was a day in Auschwitz like? What was a day in Dachau like? And I am never able to answer. Now, why can't I answer? And why can't people answer? To tell them from the heart what a day in Auschwitz was like, I have to put myself back in Auschwitz, and I am scared I won't be able to leave.'

d) Positivization of the negative

This psychic mechanism was outlined in previous observations concerning femininity and culture (Alizade, A.M. 1992, Chapter 5) in which I presented the hypothesis of a slide from negation towards affirmation. As the object in consideration remains unaffected directly, the negation, despite being a 'no' with respect to the object, does not exclude that which is positive which could affect it. In the domain of femininity, 'not having a penis' says nothing about what a woman does in fact have. The affirmation and positivization of the feminine is played out in new symbolic equations. This mental space of positivization neutralizes negative cultural connotations towards women.

The positivization of the negative can be applied to aspects of pathology following the basic hypotheses set out in this book. Psychoanalysis can help the patient access their psychic resources to free themselves from auto-destructive impulses which render them impotent. This subject is linked to the reversal of repetition.

e) Resignification and de-signification

The purpose of resignification and the gradual unravelling of meaning of the painful moments the patient has experienced is to dissolve (by means of de-signification) the active traumatic nucleus of representations and affects in the mind of the patient.

CHAPTER SEVEN

The internal setting[1]

Introduction

The setting is the formal arrangement which makes it possible to set up the kind of working atmosphere that is conducive to the psychoanalytic venture.

In focusing on the notion of 'internal setting', I am making an artificial division within the complex notion of the setting in psychoanalysis. I shall be paying particular attention to the most intimate and essential part of analytic treatment.

My interest in studying the concept of internal setting goes back several years (1982, 1996b, 1999c). I proposed the term in order to designate a certain number of elements that belong to the internal world of the analyst, to that of the patient, and to the field of action of the analysis. It is an invariant, a working apparatus built into the mind of the analyst and the atmosphere of the session. It exerts an influence on the external variables, and constitutes an organizer of the process of psychoanalytic exploration. Simply stating or presuming that it is present is not enough to bring it into existence.

[1] This chapter has been presented at the Société Psychanalytique de Paris, Rencontre APA-SPP 2002.

Similarly, it is impossible to convey adequately the richness of the internal setting in any given individual.

The internal setting raises questions about some of the standard formulations of psychoanalysis and makes it possible to draw up hypotheses concerning possible technical innovations.

The psychoanalytic setting: Acting-out and movement

'Setting' is a post-Freudian term. Freud (1913c) simply put forward some ideas for improving the efficacy of psychoanalytic work. Winnicott (1941) was one of the first to use the actual term. Lorand (1946) proposed a set of rules, but did not use the term 'setting'. Subsequent contributions have tried to establish the parameters of the setting, treating them as premises to be universally adopted. Their purpose was to lay a foundation which would ensure the objectivity and scientific nature of psychoanalysis. This work of clarification has certainly made it easier to share understanding and experience, but it has also inhibited innovation in the investigation of possible variants of psychoanalytic treatment.

The setting has thus been defined in relation to its external aspect: times; fees; frequency of sessions; holiday breaks; rules about absences and missed sessions; patient on the couch; the overall importance of speech as a medium; the open-ended duration of the treatment.

Anzieu (1990b, p. 34) answered his own question about the psychoanalytic session setting as follows: 'My response is that the setting could only have been invented by Freud, and confirmed by his successors, because it represents a homology with the topographical structure of the psychic apparatus.' In the same vein, Spitz (1965) thought that the setting imprints upon analytical work a prototype of the mother—infant relationship. It is the way in which mental life is constituted that accounts for the basic form of the setting.

In their ongoing development of the analytic contract, psychoanalysts have come to prioritize physical immobility, avoidance of physical contact, blankness of facial expression and the exclusive use of speech as the principal instruments of mental transformation.

Freud, of course, used to move around quite freely in his consulting room, the master of his own psycho-corporeal space. This makes quite a contrast with the rules followed by those analysts who have been perhaps over-concerned with the importance of speech, permitting only minimum expression through physical attitudes. There developed a psychoanalytic superego (if I may use such an expression), made up of normative conventions accepted by a consensus of psychoanalysts, in which physical immobility and a certain silent authority have been predominant. Enactment and movement, whether on the part of the analyst or on the part of the patient, have been considered as equivalent to the notion of resistance to remembering. This idea, inspired by Freud's famous 1914g paper, has been applied to an exceptional degree within the space of the session. A litany of commandments—no touching; no action; no movement—infiltrated the analyst's thinking. Keeping one's mind in a state of purity became an ideal, if not an actual rule. Psychoanalytic identity came to be constituted in the context of restricted bodily behaviour, which every trainee analyst had to accept and adapt to his or her own style and personality.

In 1905e Freud used the expression 'acting out' (*Agieren*) to designate the sudden brutal interruption of her analysis by his patient Dora. Let us emphasize from the outset that there is a huge difference between the kind of enactment that lies at the heart of transference in its various forms, and movement by the patient and by the analyst. Any enactment that is meaningful has its rightful place within the psychoanalytic material (it is a kind of free association that goes beyond language), and it can and must be analysed. Movement, by contrast, is born of bodily spontaneity, and is not necessarily interpretable. The art of a successful analysis lies in being capable of identifying the boundary between enactment and movement, in order to avoid excessive interpretation in the transference which is damaging to mental health and to progress in analytical treatment.

Contemporary transformations, the new pathologies and sociocultural changes have obliged psychoanalysts to reconsider their methods of analytical work. Insofar as the new demands do not adapt easily to the traditional setting, some analysts have explored new ways of conducting psychoanalysis without any of its specificity being lost in the process.

The construction of the internal setting

The internal setting is already implicit in the fundamental rules of free association, evenly suspended attention, and abstinence which were set out very early in Freud's work. When Bleger (1967) stated the factors that go to make up the setting, he included the role of the analyst. The word *role* is a reference to the conceptual universe of those functions of the analyst's mind that organize the main lines along which the treatment progresses.

This setting includes all the regulations and psychic processes which emanate from the analyst's ego-structures (*Ichgestaltungen*, Freud, 1923b, pp. 48, 55). It is very difficult, and to some extent impossible, to say precisely of what exactly these internal configurations consist; they are progressively created in the analyst's mind as the internalization of psychoanalysis *qua* discipline proceeds. Thus a theoretical-experiential foundation is created, upon which is installed a sort of free-floating spontaneity that is indispensable for engaging with the many obstacles that lie in the path of any analytical treatment. Within these *Gestalts*, I presume that there exists a protective superego aspect, which keeps an eye on the proper unfolding of the work of the analysis, while at the same time taking note of ongoing clinical phenomena. The construction of these functional *Gestalts* is the basis for the instrument which accompanies the analyst from within throughout that clinical work. I emphasize the term 'work', which points to a continual making of decisions and strategies in the development of any treatment, with its different transference and counter-transference vicissitudes.

I would argue that the internal setting is something 'which must exist' or 'which is absolutely necessary' for the treatment to count as true analysis. Work with the setting, whether internal or external, necessitates periodic adjustments which organize these interactions and raise fresh considerations as to its complexity.

The internal setting is the first manifestation in action, within the field of the analysis, of a *Gestalt* shared with the patient, who will internalize the internal setting all through the treatment process. The internal setting unfolds within the transference/counter-transference relationship. Thus is created a space within a sort of endopsychic, inter-subjective geography, which sustains and contains the succession of psychic events that go to make up the psychoanalytic experience.

The internal setting depends on intra-psychic factors, inter-subjective elements and communication. The construction of this space is a delicate process which results from the encounter between an analyst who possesses the internal apparatus of analysis and a patient who accepts the unfolding of the analytical work. As early as the initial interview the analyst brings this 'internal apparatus' into play as the session develops. The analyst's mind, worked on by his or her unconscious, gradually becomes capable of receiving and communicating the unconscious productions of both participants, analyst and patient.

At first, novice analysts tend either to be dependent on their supervisors or on the inflexibility of a technique that reassures them. Sometimes, with varying degrees of success, they allow themselves to be submerged by improvisations.

Little by little the internal setting improves, and becomes more refined or differentiated; this process continues throughout life, and depends on the vicissitudes of the analyst's own personal and psychoanalytic history. It is directly proportional to the analyst's passion for analysis, talent, and mental health. Psychoanalysts integrate it with the help of their own analysis, and their own experience of life, including the personal conditions with which they are confronted. Perhaps it is for this reason that Freud made a personal analysis the primary condition for becoming an analyst.

In becoming part of the analyst's person, the setting becomes an integral part of his or her presence. The analyst perceives what has not been put into words—facial expressions, tone of voice, resistance manifested through gestures. The meta-verbal field, the semiology of silence, the emotional atmosphere of each session—all these are aspects of the meta-setting involved in the construction of the internal setting.

The setting becomes a containing envelope which facilitates work on whatever it contains. Its form may vary according to many different factors: the patient's psychopathology; phase of the analysis; intrusion of reality into the treatment; crisis of ageing, and so on. The malleability of its form allows for action upon its content. The setting represents the membrane necessary for containing the drive impulses, of both analyst and patient, within a working zone which offers patients the necessary support for letting their disorders unfold without the disruption of an expulsive scansion or a brutal interruption of the session. If there is too much tension in the formal aspects, work on the content may be impaired, and in extreme cases this can become iatrogenic. The setting may, at times, require successive reorganizations. The setting may be suspended at certain moments in order for it to be re-established later. These movements of the setting oblige us to make a distinction between avoidance (desertion, acting-out by the patient), flexibility, and transitory suspension of the setting.

The internal setting becomes an instrument of understanding that is permanently on the alert so as to be able to detect what is going on in the unconscious—an invisible radar which receives the vibrations of the patient's mind. From this point of view the analyst should not worry about a transitory loss of the setting, which may be necessary; it may even trigger new growth, a time for comprehension, understanding or development in empathy with the patient at a given moment in the treatment. The internal setting allows for the possibility that elimination of certain external invariants (use of the couch; number of sessions; location of the analytic encounter) will not necessarily lead to a collapse of the internal setting or of the effectiveness of the treatment. The internal setting belongs to a phenomenology of the invisible, of an enacted perception that is not measurable by external manifestations. An external setting that is too precisely delineated may function as a useless rule or even have the iatrogenic effect of immobilization, as the *locus* of an anality derived from Thanatos. The analyst has to remain vigilant as to the negative consequences of the demands of a psychoanalytic superego ignorant of the plasticity of psychic patterns and of the dynamic nature of processes which require mental rapidity, intelligence, and creativity.

The instructions given at the beginning of the analysis as to how the work should proceed represent simply an initial flow chart that neither forbids nor avoids thinking about how the setting constantly changes (Goldberg, 2001); it is possible to re-define it, and rules that have been modified may be re-adopted. The setting itself is maintained despite these detours and modifications. This takes us back to the complexity of the problem of the structure of psychoanalytic treatment (Baranger, 1961–1962, p. 147).

The patient may challenge the external setting by questioning the fee demanded; refusing a higher frequency of sessions; asking for changes in the times of sessions; and such like. What the patient cannot do—and this is the sovereign domain of psychoanalysis—is to escape from the fact that the internal setting is brought into play and therefore will have certain consequences as its subtle, meta-psychological and object-related movements unfold.

The internal setting is an interactive, inter-subjective framework. Whether Freudian, Kleinian or Lacanian, psychoanalysts begin by affirming themselves as such. All analysts create schools of their own, even if they profess to belong to a particular persuasion. In the depths of their being they are unique: perhaps without knowing it, each analyst is unique. The only analytic potential they have is what they have been able to sediment—through castration—in a vital, ever-present movement. This idea implies that each 'becomes a psychoanalyst' in a changing manner over the years.

Like the pans on a pair of scales, the internal setting leans mainly to the analyst's side at the start of the treatment, and then, as the analytic process is gradually established, the special art of each analyst and the singularity of each patient modify this equilibrium. Patients bring into play their own 'analytic vocation' or 'analytic sails', and internalize the internal setting: their unconscious becomes conscious, they come to experience their resistances and defences, and they will have moments of self-analysis. The creation of the internal setting will enrich the unconscious links which bind the analytic couple together and will enhance the effectiveness of the analytic alchemy. It will be weakened by negative reactions and impasses in the treatment.

The psychic properties of the internal setting interact like radars or invisible antennae. They can be listed as follows: 1) listening with the third ear; 2) permeability of the analyst to his or her own unconscious and that of the patient; 3) evenly suspended attention; 4) free association by the analyst and by the patient; 5) observance of the interactive rules of play; and 6) spontaneity and creativity.

Listening with the 'third ear'

This third ear includes listening to 'interior voices' (Reik, 1926, p. 26), to what is not expressed in words, to subliminal messages that spring from the depths of the unconscious. The dimension of the inaudible and of the domain beyond speech is part of this listening. Working with silence and the extensive field of the affects, the parameters of which do not lend themselves to formalization, constitutes a non-representational field in which the elements that lie outside speech possess a semiology of their own (Fliess, 1949).

Permeability of the analyst to his or her own unconscious and that of the patient

Freud (1912–1913, 1915e) wrote of the existence of communication from one unconscious to another, but he did not elaborate on the issue. The deployment of the internal setting requires a capacity in the analyst to connect with the patient's unconscious and to reach analytic empathy within the transference/counter-transference relationship, which all the time remains imprecise and impossible to categorize. This may include the analyst's capacity for investigating the patient's experience. The analyst becomes a kind of translator of what remains illegible, a sort of scientific diviner. We can relate this to the 'total internal response' (Racker, 1959, p. 97), which has to do with empathy towards the patient.

Evenly suspended attention

As a psychoanalytic attitude, evenly suspended attention switches on the 'invisible radar' of the internal setting. Open and relaxed listening captures the productions of the unconscious and temporarily suspends ideology and principles which prevent listening.

Free association by the patient and by the analyst. This idea implies the creative freedom of the analyst's thought, unlimited by breaks or inhibitions due to the workings of the superego. In the associations triggered by the material, and in the patient's free associations, the analyst finds new significant clues, thanks to the bridge that is established with the patient's archaic dreams, with the material of earlier sessions and of various memories. Memory comes and goes between representation and affect, with full freedom to associate, to create hypotheses, constructions, and tentative interpretations.

Observance of the interactive rules of play, such as those concerning abstinence and neutrality.

Spontaneity and creativity. The internal setting requires spontaneity of reflection combined with a *corpus* of internalized rules. Spontaneity is achieved as soon as the analyst is past the first stages of training with their inevitable element of idealization and projection of knowledge. Creativity plays by itself. Analysts throws themselves into the lake of their analytical intuitions and swim in the waters of their internal sea, kept afloat by the process of training which constitutes their psychoanalytic upbringing. They liberate themselves from the injunctions received from their various supervisors or from theoretical texts full of certitudes. The external setting can also be dissolved in the spontaneity of the situation, but it remains firmly held together by the internal setting. The optimal distance in the analyst—patient exchange depends on the level of the setting. The analyst becomes a decipherer and an inventor. He or she is a scientist and, to some extent, an artist. The work of the analysis becomes playful, even at the most difficult times when negative reactions invade the session, when the defiance which is set in motion by the work becomes a passionate adventure.

Final thoughts

The essence of psychoanalysis is what takes place in the internal setting, in the field of internal worlds that get to know each other, that interpenetrate each other, and of which one—that of the analyst—brings on to the terrain of language the partly ineffable processes of representations, affects and silences.

The analyst's creativity adapts and softens the external framework of the setting at specific moments and in specific situations in each analysis. One has to keep in mind the possibility that it may be necessary to modify the external setting significantly in order to keep the analytic process going. In such a situation, the external setting, even though it is the depositary of psychotic anxieties (Bleger, 1967), has to be formally dismantled in order to maintain a basis without which the analysis cannot proceed.

If an analyst, because of private difficulties or an excess of analytical blindness, establishes a strict external setting but at the same time an insufficient internal setting, the analysis will no doubt be useful as a certain kind of catharsis or holding situation, but mutative and elaborative results will be poor or even non-existent. The external setting will be no more than a sort of empty framework for a useless apparatus. On the other hand, when the analysis develops with a flexible external setting accompanied by a sustained rhythm of unconscious communication and transference discoveries by means of interpretations and constructions, the possibility of success is increased.

CHAPTER EIGHT

Reanalysis and impasse

Reanalysis

The word *reanalysis* refers to new analysis or 'more' analysis. Previous treatment may have finished or have been interrupted for various reasons.

The influence of the previous analysis persists in the post-analysis, thanks to the effects of the analytical process that the ex-analysand has internalized. Self-analysis and post-analysis are interlinked and contribute to the maintenance and the improvement of the state of well-being that has been achieved.

Every patient has their analytical history: number of analysts, years in analysis, results of the analysis, unresolved transferences, disappointments, suffering caused by the iatrogenic effects of analysis, idealizations and so on and so forth.

At a certain point, the symptoms reoccur and new problems related to the patient's vitality lead the ex-patient to ask for a consultation. The patient experiences the need to restart their analysis (with the same analyst or a different one). The demand returns. The hope emerges of bringing about an unexpected change. The patient brings to their analysis the transferences inherited from past analysis. It is not uncommon to find resentment on the part of the patient against an analyst who they hold responsible for not obtaining positive results. Whose fault is it that their suffering has returned so quickly? Is this a bad patient or was the previous analyst incapable? Why, after many long years of analysis, has the narcissistic conflict still not been resolved, or why does the patient still have difficulty in finding a partner or being successful at work?

In Argentina, a middle-aged patient who asks for a consultation for reanalysis has usually been in analysis previously for a long period of time: fifteen, twenty years.

Although the analysis is interminable, after 20 years of analysis, it is expected that the main problems of the patient will have been resolved.

In some cases, it seems reasonable to wonder if there was not an excess of analysis and a certain iatrogenesis. This may be due to the continuance of countless sessions of unelaborated pain, or the analysis blocking the potentiality of the patient's vitality by focusing the interpretations exclusively on the sick areas of the psyche. This may have intensified the pathology and the resistance to change which, in turn, could have fomented the impoverishment of the psyche due to the defensive repetition of monotonous, empty discourse in the service of the death-instinct (psychic death).

Different types of demand for reanalysis exist. These range from the genuine desire to restart a long period of analysis and to obtain more benefits from this technique, to the desire to have sporadic analytical interviews (at the most once a week). In the latter case, the analyst's role is to collaborate with the patient in their own self-analysis.

The demand is particularly difficult when the psychic structure of the patient displays symptoms, demonstrating the need to resolve a form of psychic functioning which is seemingly irreducible. If others have not been successful, why should this new analyst achieve a positive outcome? The analyst is faced with a challenge, above all, when the patient brings with them hostile transferences and unconscious vindictive feelings to the analysis. The patient comes to their sessions asking the impossible, disrupting and damaging the analytical setting and hindering the work of the chosen analyst.

It is time to draw up a sort of 'analytical map'. Did working-through take place at any point in the previous treatment? What were the main complexes that were analysed? Was there an impasse during this analysis? If so, how did it manifest itself?

The analyst is not taken in by the manifest discourse of the patient and puts forward a hypothesis, for example, that the patient has little potential for working-through and that in previous treatment either the holding function or the bastion created by the patient's resistances was the predominant factor.

Will the patient have analytical treatment again? What form will the setting take?

The study of the mental functioning of this new patient will come to a standstill in those areas which are resistant to working-through. The analyst must not be taken in by the charming outer appearance that the patient may present.

In reanalysis, the new analysis picks up where the previous analysis left off and at the same time a new bond is created.

For sure, there will already exist certain associative pathways which have already exhausted their elaborative potential.

The analyst must use their creative potential to the full. This creativity challenges the conventional psychoanalytical setting and provides a stimulus for psychoanalytical investigation.

It can be predicted that analysis will encounter difficulties stemming from the irreducibility of a symptom or a character trait. New lines of approach are sought both in terms of the pathology and the health of the patient. The habitual symptom is not given too much attention to avoid boring and retraumatizing the patient. Psychic fatigue can occur when the same worn-out associative pathways are revisited.

A reanalysis can become the first genuine analysis and the first time the patient has had a corrective emotional experience[1] with profound effects.

Impasse and its variants

The phenomena of impasse and of interruption over the course of analysis impact on the unconscious and the dynamic of the transference-counter-transference.

---

[1]'Corrective emotional experience' is an expression attributed to Enrique Pichon Rivière.

Impasse is a French word which signifies 'standstill', 'blind alley' or 'dead end'. This constitutes a vicissitude during the psychoanalytical process.

The weakening (often transitory) of the demand provides a space for a psychic period of impasse.

The analyst listens and perceives that the analysis has come to a halt and that the production of material and the transferential process has ceased. Ethically the analyst is forced to consider that this may not be the time to interrupt the patient's treatment and may need to refer the patient to another analyst or simply steer the analysis to quiet waters while waiting for the winds which will set in motion the demand once again.

During the period of impasse, work is carried out by the analyst. It is necessary to review the trajectory of the treatment, study the clinical stage which the patient is at, examine the countertransference and plan a strategy aimed at generating the impetus to steer the analysis in a new direction.

I do not consider a priori that impasse is something negative. The exploration of the impasse will undoubtedly give rise to clinical material relating to repression, which has resisted coming to the surface. Respect for this defence mechanism, understood to be a necessary protection of the psyche, requires that the analyst proceeds calmly and cautiously.

On 'listening to' the impasse from its different angles, it is important not to lose sight of the interminability of analysis and the importance of psychic activity, of which transferential impasse or interruption is no more than yet another avatar. The analyst-observer must avoid the danger of 'creating' that which is observed (Pragier G. and Faure-Pragier. S., 1990) and should themselves assume a certain 'psychic exile' (Nasio, J.D. 1980) enabling them to break new ground.

This underlying hypothesis is in line with the paradigm of chaotic, unpredictable determinism. This is at odds with linearity, in which there is a fixed idea that is fervently adhered to, this being that it is always beneficial to continue with specific analytical treatment and that there is always a need to be in analysis.

I will distinguish between three types of impasse.

1) Impasse at the outset of analysis

The threshold of analysis proves difficult to cross. A brief foray into analysis is made so that the patient can quickly withdraw within their inner defences. This is related to a pseudo-beginning of the analysis and a pseudo-demand. This phenomenon is closely linked to the diagnosis of the analysability of the patient. This impasse at the outset of treatment destroys the possibility of the existence of a genuine demand and, as a consequence, analysis cannot take place.

2) Resistential impasse

This takes place over the course of the analytical treatment. In this case, 'the failure is not visible and the treatment continues' (Etchegoyen, H. 1986) at the hands of the patient and their resistances. This is manifested in the form of 'repetitive cycles of verbal acting-outs' often connected to the bad faith of the patient (Maldonado, J. 1975).

This type of impasse occurs during analysis (analysis in impasse, or analysis when the analytical process is not actually taking place), or results in the interruption of analysis. It is the impasse caused by stagnation or by resistances. At this point, the concept of 'bastion', coined by W. and M. Baranger, comes into play (Baranger, W., and Baranger, M. 1961–1962, 1964).

3) Impasse of detachment

The psychoanalytical impasse displays a positive side when previous analytical work has focused on psychic elaboration and the uncovering of unconscious production. A time of quiescence comes about. The subject reorganizes their inner world now 'without outside help' and without off-loading their conflicts onto the analyst. The patient's self-analysis and post-analysis have their own forward momentum. Or there may be a de-analysis of the patient, by which I mean a certain lack of understanding or disinterest in their psychic functioning.

In this period of psychic quiescence, the subject recovers from the effects of the unconscious interchange. This psychic activity, which inevitably takes place over the passage of time, can either consolidate the impasse or produce a *'reinitiation of analysis'* with the resultant reinitiation of the demand. The analytical function promotes this pattern, namely 'impasse—reinitiation of analysis', having a liberating effect. Analytical freedom is an essential element for the creativity of analysis and also for maintaining the openness of psychoanalytical listening. The desire to analyse must be rekindled session after session otherwise there is a risk of analysis becoming insipid, which Freud discussed with Blanton (Blanton, S. 1930).

In his work on analysis terminable and interminable, Freud (1937c, p. 222) talks in depth about the complexities of the ending of analysis, which must always be dealt with cautiously given that the patient is still exposed to the risk of contracting 'a second illness', despite the successful outcome of a first analysis, if fate is unkind and life proves difficult.

The impasse of detachment is not synonymous with the end of analysis but rather constitutes one more avatar of the psyche's analytical trajectory.

An excess of analysis under unfavourable conditions can prove iatrogenic. The concept of 'respect for resistances' goes hand in hand with this particular concept of impasse. The analytical impasse, in so far as the mind is in a state of rest while the work of the unconscious takes place, does not mean that the process of elaboration has broken down, as in the case of the resistential impasse. The impasse is observed with calm. The 'positive impasse' becomes a type of return to oneself and an acceptance of personal limits.

The 'impasse of detachment' results in a disorganization of the psyche, but in a positive sense given that it opens the door to new organizational structures in the heart of this apparent disorganization (Pragier G. & Faure-Pragier. S., 1990). It is a mental movement occurring within a multiplicity of psychic avatars.

As regards the positive aspect of the impasse of detachment, new configurations of dynamic understanding are created together with a concept of effectiveness of analysis which lies outside conventional parameters.

Reflections on unconscious functioning in the light of the psychoanalytic impasse

Freud discovered the structure of the unconscious, a discovery which has provided the theoretical-clinical framework of psychoanalysis. To the repressed unconscious is added the unconscious proper, which is inextricably bound to the soma. This sustains, by autonomasia, a place for the unknown, in close parallel with the famous navel of the dream (Freud, S. 1900a). Later, Freud (1915e) writes: 'Everything that is repressed must remain unconscious but we must state at the very outset that the repressed does not cover everything that is unconscious. The unconscious has the wider compass: the repressed is a part of the unconscious' (p. 166).

The repressed unconscious of the infant is structured in relation to a fellow human being who enables it to be reborn into the world of language. The encounter with an other and the gestation of the unconscious are closely linked. On the one hand, the unconscious is order, governed by its own laws and on the other, it is disorder and chaos. Freud (1933a), when speaking about the id says: 'We approach the id with analogies: we call it a chaos, a cauldron full of seething excitations. We picture it as being open at its end to somatic influences, and as there taking up into itself instinctual needs which find their psychological expression in it' (p. 73).

When a patient and an analyst meet, they do so within the framework of preconscious phenomena. Unconscious transmission (Freud, S. 1913i, 1915e) between the two individuals occupies a primordial space. Transference neurosis is played out in the unconscious dyadic field of interaction between both participants in the analytical adventure. Affects, experiences, non-verbal transmission make up the axes of force of this dynamic which sustains the work of analysis. What is established is a sort of interlacement between the unconscious of two individuals generating a psychoanalytic field which enables, by means of a fertile interchange between the stream of the patient's associations and the analyst's interpretations, transmission from one unconscious to the other.

The demand for analysis is the call of the unconscious of a subject who is suffering from certain symptoms, and who is in search of another individual who can lend them their own unconscious functioning to take away these symptoms. This interlacement between the unconscious of two individuals can abruptly come to halt when a strong resistance gives rise to a negative therapeutic reaction. The patient withdraws from analysis managing to arrest the analytical process within their sessions and later by interrupting their treatment. The transferential impasse has taken hold.

I will put forward a hypothesis to explain the impasse related to detachment: the psychic network of pathways generated in the field of transference can become saturated. *The saturation of unconscious pathways* is related to the limits of the analyst, their inevitable blind spots and the very dynamic of psychoanalysis which 'exhausts', in certain circumstances, the source of the stream of associations which can lead to the curative effects of working-through. The analytical process comes to a stop. Phenomenologically, this state comes about as a result of fatigue and boredom with analysis. Knowledge stagnates and the demand and creativity deteriorate. The 'seething cauldron' of the id has stilled in its interchange with the unconscious of the analyst.

CHAPTER NINE

Clinical vignettes

In these pages I will present some clinical vignettes to exemplify the process of working with positivity. I have selected certain stages in the analysis and the analytical psychotherapy of various patients, fully aware that written transmission can never truly reflect the complexity of positivity and that its in-depth study of positivity requires further investigation.

The multiplicity of mental configurations and interchanges which occur over the course of analysis make it difficult to delimit with total accuracy the effect of the positive, as distinct from other factors, in the analytical process. Nonetheless, these brief clinical sketches illustrate the clinical application of the ideas I have expressed.

Celeste

The patient agreed to begin reanalysis after having initially undergone treatment when she was young, around seventeen years old. She manifested signs of having benefited from her treatment although the basic nucleus of her suffering, which consisted of a depression based on hypochondriac elements, had not changed.

In successive sessions, she returned time and time again to her childhood and adolescent traumas (amongst other pathogenic elements being exile, moving from one place to another, and being constantly belittled by her parents). Sessions always included liberal mention of her multiple physical ailments—dyspepsia, tachycardia, menstrual pain—for which she was consulting different medical specialists.

The atmosphere in the sessions was one of sadness and apathy. Celeste appeared to be in a state of psychic survival and her external successes, namely having created a harmonious family situation, did not help dispel her moodiness, her irritability, or her dissatisfaction with her fate. The clinical material arising from the session seemed like a masturbatory, masochistic rumination.

She never missed a session, which enabled the creation of a protective covering of positivity in the analytical field, facilitating the expression of negative transference but without this becoming a destructive acting-out.

After two years of little progress, I requested the advice of a colleague to evaluate the need for medication. This professional, in an in-depth interview, asked her if perhaps her chronic suffering depended on 'not having explored her conflicts and trauma to the degree which they warranted'. His opinion was that the patient was not in need of medication of any kind.

Celeste did not like the psychiatrist. She expressed her despair in the face of the failure of the psychoanalytical treatment and experienced a profound feeling of hopelessness.

I decided to change the course of the treatment. I focused on the positive transference which is real (Greenson, R. and Wexler, M. 1969) and the interchange of vital energy between both analyst and analysand. I opened a new psychic window of exploration, and let the symptomatic area lie without exacerbating it by further work with associations.

In some sessions, we worked on her conflictive nuclei, but in others I did not respond to the closed, monotonous discourse resulting from her resistances. Certain associative residues provided the means of joining together some untraumatic and often insignificant life experiences. *Trophic insignificance* provided the opportunity to break new associative ground. My observations and questions were directed towards these representational-affective complexes.

Celeste learnt that 'we can also talk about this' and incorporated this reflection about her non-conflictive thoughts into her associations. The valuing of pleasurable experiences, conveyed via interpretations, gradually taught her the value of small, pleasant, everyday events.

The chronic *associative retraumatization* gave way to a psychic lightness thanks to the detraumatizing process which was taking place. This lightening of the psychic burden uncovered a healthy part of the psyche which had been, until this point, buried beneath the weight of the neurotic-thanatic nucleus. Gradually, a state of *transferential good-health* became established. The deneurotization, on this occasion, was reached indirectly, and was the result of the intensification and strengthening of healthy areas of the psyche.

Silvia

Silvia was in an overt state of complete helplessness: trembling, crying, she felt totally lost. She had been in mourning for more than a year after the death of a close relative.

The clinical diagnosis was of a dependent, infantile personality within a phobic structure.

She was a virgin and in her late thirties. The social pressure to marry and have children strengthened her schizoid mechanisms of defence. Silvia avoided going to social gatherings and closed herself away at home, only leaving her house to go to work. This crisis was exacerbated when she was made redundant from work. With no money and no friends, she considered herself a burden on her family. She felt as if she had not achieved anything in her life and that she was a living failure.

Silvia's phobia of sex limited her job opportunities. She feared possible harassment by a senior member of staff and even having to participate in conversations between colleagues where 'a subject related to sex always comes up'.

She was in analysis for three years before coming to see me. She had tried, during this time, to have a sexual experience, which had turned out to be a total failure and had only served to increase her defences and to confirm her belief that sex was not for her. At times, this anguish reached a level which was debilitating. She had also had a therapeutic experience with a psychiatrist, who had tried to encourage her to lose her physical inhibitions.

I observed the repetition of scenarios, which were distressing and limiting, and her consequent defensive withdrawal.

Silvia often cried during the sessions, repeating, 'I can't.' She would then stare intently into my eyes, in pregnant silence. She made associations relating to her childhood and her adolescence, when she had been excluded at school and had low self-esteem. At a party when she was twelve years old a young boy had invited her to dance and had taken her arm. Silvia had fled, uttering a scream of terror. After this incident she had never allowed herself to be touched by a man.

The sessions continued. There were some signs of working-through with consequent psychic relief. However, the basic problem still persisted and appeared to be of an irreducible nature.

Concomitantly, I explored early, positive memories. I searched for events in her past where I could fix or anchor pleasurable experiences which had happened repeatedly. I was interested in the complemental series which could account for her low self-esteem.

I worked with 'what is possible' and also with 'what there was'. Any attempt to encourage her 'genitality' at this stage of her mental organization would have been out of the question.

The atmosphere in the sessions was revitalized by encouraging Silvia to discuss her plans and projects for the future, no matter how humble or small they were. From her phobic condition, her greatest desire was to win the lottery to have enough money never to work again. These fantasies were explored with great sensitivity and respect for the boundaries of her psychic defences. Within the therapeutic alliance, Silvia's suffering eased by working through the social, marital demands she had projected onto me. 'Nobody is pressuring you'; 'It's ok if you're not able to'; 'This is permitted.'

What developed within Silvia was a sense of ownership of herself (Alizade, A.M. 1999). She gradually cut out for herself a 'psychic skin' and discovered that she could exercise her right to be alone in society. She reaffirmed her self-esteem: 'This is how I am.'

The process of strengthening her self-esteem was accompanied with affective changes. She experienced fleeting moments of happiness and allowed herself a weak smile during the sessions.

In the two years which followed, her improvement was consolidated.

Carlos

Carlos was young and said little. The sessions, almost silent, provided a protective covering of positivity. Associations were few and his attendance at the sessions was constant. He came 'to be in the session'.

Gradually, he worked through some basic conflicts such as his resentment towards his father, who had abandoned him when he was five years old.

Together we reconstructed a small part of his life history. In an atmosphere of basic trust and of quiet opening up, Carlos made progress. He graduated from university, he found a well-paid job, and he married.

The sessions were essentially happy and calm. The analyst became the 'new transferential object' with whom he could construct a positive, new human relationship which he had never experienced before.

There was an abundance of good humour in the sessions and Carlos developed a sense of reconciliation with his internal objects along with an improved sense of psychic well-being.

The patient consolidated the positive gains made during the early years of his analysis. Nevertheless, in parallel, there persisted a phobic attitude which prevented him from progressing in the workplace. He had mixed feelings about becoming a father and manifested a defensive, psychic levity which enabled him to avoid exploring his inner world.

Carlos continued with his treatment, where everything was seemingly resolved. Only now is he in a position to try to understand in greater depth his childhood and adolescent conflicts. A new stage of analysis has begun. Within the protective surround of positivity, the tears began to fall: the reopening of unfinished mourning for a relative, his nocturnal terror on hearing his parents argue, a negative experience at school. The traumatic thrived during this period of psychic self-containment. The state of transferential good health achieved previously made room for new forms of transference neurosis.

Margarita

This patient exhibited symptoms of chronic suffering. The successive affairs of her husband with different secretaries and friends of the patient had crushed her self-esteem. The depression and anxiety which was manifested prevented her from doing any task which could have afforded her gratification. She would spend long hours lying on her bed, shrouded in the cigarette smoke of her room, apathetic and devoid of hope.

The feeling of abandonment was revived and relived through the infidelity of her husband. Margarita had no desire to live. The fulfillment of her duties as a mother required a great deal of effort.

She resisted analysis in its traditional sense and accepted a setting of two weekly sessions face-to-face.

An in-depth analysis of her life history revealed a history of orphanages, rape and mourning.

Despite slow progress and the need to overcome resistances, I managed to reach the nucleus of her conflicts. In parallel, I salvaged some pleasurable experiences from her history, such as successes in her childhood and dreams which she had realized. I did not focus on or afford primacy to traumatic clinical material. Quite the contrary: there came a time in her treatment when the associations of the patient were gradually replaced by new life projects and expectations—doing gym, taking up a new artistic activity, and so forth.

The strengthening of healthy parts of the psyche sustained it in its vulnerability.

Margarita blossomed. She reinitiated her profession and managed to partially distance herself from the dramas of her life, concentrating on her life projects. She developed an inner, creative space. This inner transformation attracted the attention of her partner, who gradually gravitated towards her.

The treatment succeeded in curing the psychic disability of the patient, enabling her to enjoy life.

Ines

Ines, a young patient, came for a consultation as a result of an anxiety crisis. For her, to be analysed was synonymous with removing that part of the past which was linked to suffering and negativity.

She wanted to get through this phase quickly. She was intelligent and extremely capable in terms of working-through her problems. Her analysis, characterized by an ambivalent transference and a strong resistance against free association, was a slow process with many obstacles. However, at the end of a few years, her sexuality had flourished and her anxiety had notably diminished.

Ines expressed the desire to stop her treatment as she considered that she had spent too much time stirring up painful memories and conflicts. Her new approach to life predisposed her to periods where she experienced heightened feelings of well-being. The focus of the closing stage of her analysis consisted in consolidating the positive gains made over the course of her treatment. The patient felt relieved when I made it explicit that analysis did not only involve revisiting unbearable memory traces but rather that working with feelings of well-being was also an integral part of the process. What followed were months of intense work where she relived childhood experiences and strengthened her positive identifications with grandparents and great-grandparents. She forgave mistakes in her upbringing, overcame resentment against her primary objects and developed her ability to enjoy each day. When free-association touched on a painful memory, it was incorporated into her associations without masochistic fixations.

Roberto

The therapeutic process consisted of raising his awareness of the difficulties he had in deepening his understanding of his psychic life. In an extended period of pre-analysis, I managed to obtain a small amount of clinical material relating to his childhood memories. He did not dream and associated in a way which was obsessively controlled. His identity as a busy, high-powered business executive served to create a bastion of resistances.

The psychoanalytical focus was on developing the healthy parts of his psyche. Whilst respecting the boundaries of his psychic defences, I made interpretations which increased the permeability of his unconscious. The physical risk to which he was exposed due to the stress he suffered at work was the focus of my observations and interpretations. Little by little, his symptoms decreased and he began to express an interest in having a better understanding of himself. I observed the attenuation of the rigour of his superego and a notable improvement in the quality of his life.

CHAPTER TEN

An essay on joy

Introduction

This essay is like a major chord sounding in a book that resolutely intends, through all its pages, to give the category of positivity its rightful place in clinical work and in the theory of technique.

Joy is not included in the psychoanalytic vocabulary, and perhaps the reason is that it evokes excess. Joy radiates unboundedness.

Being joyful is a special mental state. People who are full of joy are attractive to their fellow human beings, who would like to be infected by their cheerfulness or to share in this vital energy. It is an affect that makes thought lighter. It has its roots in the happy experiences of early childhood, in the harmony between complementary series, and in the free flow of the life-drive.

The close examination of happy moments is of great interest to the analyst along the path towards a cure. Joy is in itself a potential source of health that should be carefully explored, both clinically and meta-psychologically.

The first love-object (the mother or her substitute) is, under favourable conditions, one that gives joy and pleasure and is transformed into an *affectively positive object*. The quality of affects which develop in the primary object-*infans* bond give rise to a sensory-affective matrix, providing a basic substrate of good or poor health. A happy family and a harmonious environment are stabilizing and facilitating elements that lead to experiences of well-being. The *non-traumatic atmosphere* generated by the interaction between the mother, the father, siblings, caregivers, the social situation, and so on, provides multiple satisfactory experiences to the subjects in their inter-communication.

Play and creativity expand joy. A healthy dose of aggression adds to it and enhances it when creative play is successful. The child becomes a safe haven in which anxieties are calmed and happiness can thrive. In fantasy and in the arts (a substitute for play and a space for creativity), the adult will also find there those spaces of freedom which needed to prevent multiple sources of unpleasure from prevailing.

When confronting the world's inclemency, joy is a psychic balm. The mind is soothed and initiates psychic activity that will put an end to some repressions, albeit fleetingly. The exhausting excesses of representation are suspended. Joy sweeps off *pathogenic hyper-representations* and agrees to a truce against the repetitive insistence of neurotic thought, which is immersed in conflict. Daily life becomes a festivity: the game of joy has begun.

This is usually accompanied by an outer manifestation, such as a smile or laughter. On other occasions, it operates as a silent inner melody. It radiates into mind and body as an enlivening flow of energy from its basic core. It is transmitted per se through a body attitude, the brightness of a glance, a gesture, all of which are bodily signs of joy. The senses absorb happy experiences from the sensorial world and then outwardly express them. Joy presents itself knowing that it is unique.

It has been given many names: sentiment, emotion, affect, a set of accumulated satisfactory experiences, delight. In its pathological guise, it has been called mania, hypomania or pseudo-joy.

It can be projected onto a visible object or a causal situation (a child's graduation, a birthday gift), or it can lack any manifest object, in which case that which produces joy is unseen and unconscious.

Joy is the opposite of melancholy. While in melancholy 'the shadow of the object fell upon the ego' (Freud, 1917e, p. 249), in joy it is *the light of the object* which falls upon it. The ego thrives in the nameless pleasure generated by conscious and unconscious objects.

A joyful person is committed to the life-drive.

Cheer cheers us up. In a sort of reflex feedback loop falling back on one's own self, cheerful people are happy with the joy they may produce both in themselves and in others. Joy meets the profound human need for happiness. In all their superficiality, joy, trivial banter, shared jokes, the mere fact of feeling uplifted by being in the presence of another person, are powerful balms against anxiety and other unpleasant affects. The energy of joyfulness sweeps away sadness with its overwhelming force.

A joyous family infuses a sense of future well-being in their offspring. A family's potential health is measured by its capacity to overcome transgenerational difficult times. Sometimes, a person succeeds in freeing him or herself from the nightmares they have lived through in the past, creating a joyful atmosphere in the family—half-spontaneously, half-intentionally by dint of discipline and force of will –so as to open up a new, vital horizon for their children.

The tragic condition of the human being often makes it difficult to perceive the power this sentiment has in overcoming suffering.

Under its superficial appearance, joy has an ethical responsibility to fulfill. Aristotle said that, 'Ethics is a practical science based on common sense—that is, on the righteous judgment of good and virtuous men—showing us the life style that is needed to achieve happiness, which is the Good par excellence.'[1]

Some centuries later, Spinoza (1987, p. 235) defined the three basic affects: (1) desire, a conscious effort to persevere and to augment the potency of the human being; (2) joy, a step taken by man to progress from a lesser to a greater state of perfection; and (3) sadness, which was, conversely, a step taken from a greater to a lesser state of perfection. Spinoza said that joy is a kind of passion by which the soul advances to greater perfection (degree of reality) by increasing the body's potential action. Thus, joyfulness becomes an instrument for measuring the degree of perfection of the human soul.

[1] Quoted by Fullat and Gomis (1984, pp. 12–13).

Joy sweeps routine away and is magical: it transforms one thing into another, it surprises and it feeds the imagination. From the joyful person's top hat an improvised joke emerges, and there is laughter, gentle expressions, smiling eyes, outstretched hands. Joy is a warm gesture of solidarity.

The creation of joy is an art. Only a few, those that are able to reach the high peaks of pleasure, have this gift. These 'creators of joy' are very much appreciated. How often do we want to approach a cheerful person in search of that energizing and life-enhancing contact that can help us to cope with distress? From simple people who enjoy each instant of their life with jokes and laughter, to the very wise ones, all of them are tacitly thanked for giving their fellow beings the opportunity to experience this feeling.

In the same way that the sad person punishes those who, willingly or unwillingly, surround them, the joyful one rewards those who are near with a supreme gift, so expensive as to be priceless: good humour, pure and simple. This affect knows how to circumvent the sad spaces it comes across: it automatically minimizes them and finds their positive side.

How do you attain joy when you do not have it? Working towards happiness is always artificial and is a journey fraught with constant failure. Joy 'shall be added unto you'.[2] A clear conscience and the force of human effort in overcoming and/or accepting fate collaborate together in its creation.

A basic belief in the goodness of everything and everyone, and an optimistic outlook on life are the prerequisites of the joyful state of mind. A benevolent world welcomes the exultant emergence of joy. At the opposite extreme, bitterness is the expression of evil in its broadest sense: evil which is crystallized in a harmful world view that turns against oneself. Dreams are absent, objects disappoint us, life is sad.

The human being fluctuates between alienation and freedom. When an individual cultivates a routine way of living, tries to selfishly reach their goals and works solely for self-preservation, joy fades. Dis-alienation, as well as the retrieval of a refreshing freedom and emotion, provide the germ of all joy. When life puts

---

[2] 'Seek ye first the kingdom of God and His righteousness, and all these things **shall be added unto you**' (Matthew, 6: 33).

on the clothes of the human comedy, the individual automatically preserves a psychic distance, enabling them to view life as a drama.

Joy is usually short-lived. 'After having been liberated, human consciousness subjects itself to the imperatives of the "objective world" again and resumes an enslaving alienation' (Monedero, 1970, p. 39). However, joyful people do not give in; they defend their cheerfulness and their unerring belief in the triumph of good while feeling grateful for the fleeting moments of happiness they have experienced. Their happiness resides within themselves and they invoke it from the depths of their emotions. Cheerful human beings are the enviable owners of an invisible power.

Once free from the neurosis of society's malaise, the individual can withstand and surmount dissatisfaction and the anxiety of death armed with the happiness and positivity of everyday life. It is as if they had internalized Omar Khayyam's beautiful verses: 'Think it over: you might not be here ... So, now that you are here ... enjoy!' The benevolent superego invites good humour and even demands that ... few demands are made. This paradoxical demand of being non-demanding brings with it mental calm.

There is a dose of deception in joy. A meta-physical veil covers the harsh, painful reality of human beings who are exposed undefended to the elements. The dimension of horror remains suspended, ignored. But joy cannot negate itself, and though the person knows all too well the tragic sagas of our species, with all their painful repercussions, the authority and strength of joy triumph supreme.

Joy is positivity in its pure, unadulterated state. It can be robbed from us using wicked tricks, but it will return from its unconscious roots. With its small strength, awaiting nothing and powerless to create, it is self-sustaining and freely pours into the external world.

Among its meta-psychological faces, there is a wise, laughing superego, consubstantiated with psychical maturity and the relativity of existence.

Pathological kinds of joy

a) Pseudo-joy

Pseudo-joy manifests itself in disproportionate, wild laughter, a forced happiness that must be differentiated from the joy of maturity and from the peaceful joy that does not boast of itself. This false joy conceals feelings of shame and spite. Hidden behind the pretence of happiness, there is suffering. Joy manifests itself as a defence, a protective mask to conceal narcissistic pain.

As the poet Juana de Ibarbourou wrote:

> I have laughed so much,
> so much, that tears came to my eyes,
> so much, that on my lips a frozen smile
> remains, the fatigue of my mad laughter.

A guilty conscience, vanity, and arrogance are the source of a cheerful masquerade, where, as T.S. Eliot said in one of his poems, people take delight 'in the sty of contentment'. When joy has no ethical grounds, it is built on usurpation, corruption, and pretence.

b) Destructive joy: mania and hypomania

Here the ego blithely subjects itself to the destructive impositions of the superego. Manic triumph has a façade of cheerfulness behind which there are guilty feelings and unconscious wishes of self-destruction.

'The mania, or, if you prefer, the manic response, is the ego's masochistic delight in accomplishing acts that lead it to submit to the destructive triumph of the superego' (Garma, A. and E., 1973, p. 112). The happiness of the manic individual comes from the masochistic pleasure they get when seeing themselves destroyed, or when observing sadistically the destruction of the hated object. This kind of joy is linked to the feeling of destructive envy.

With destructive joy, the same economic conditions prevailing in melancholy are present. 'The impression which several psychoanalytic investigators have already put into words is that the content of the mania is no different from that of melancholia, that both disorders are wrestling with the same "complex", but that probably in melancholia the ego has succumbed to the complex whereas in mania it has mastered it or pushed it aside' (Freud, 1917e, p. 254).

The destructive character of this kind of joy is manifest in the accompanying excitation, and in the lack of an organized chain of thoughts. When a person is in a manic state, their associations flow incessantly, uncontrolled, and they must fight against the subjugating unconscious object.

c) Psychopathy, perversion, and wickedness

Both psychopathy and perversion are usually related to wickedness. To psychopaths, what matters is to reach their goal of using the object. Lacking an adequate superego, they are prevented from feeling sympathy, compassion or pity for the fellow human being they have harmed. On the contrary, they are glad to have achieved their end—a successful fraud, or such like.

When perversion is driven by wickedness, the malevolent behaviour of the pervert very often annihilates the other's joy forever. It is highly unlikely that the psyche is able to cope with historical or familial experiences of horror. Some areas of the psyche, affected by unforgettable trauma, remain there as a malignant cyst. Evil bears fruit: the sadistic joy of the destructive other obliterates the potential happiness of the victim. It is extraordinarily difficult—though not impossible—to recover from these experiences.

Clinical reflections

a) The joyful mother

By 'joyful mother' I mean the mother who transmits positive feelings and the life-drive to her children. She not only gives them bodily life, but also psychical life. The joyful mother possesses the basic joy of all healthy people.

Her joy is both the evidence and the result of transgenerational and individual experiences of happiness. It is not unlikely that she is part of a generational chain of people that are essentially good humoured. The possession of joy is a luxury, precisely because it is a priceless possession. The mother who is affectively a joyful object becomes a *disseminator of health.*

The child receives the mother's libidinal and object blessings via the dyadic body-affect interaction. This kind of mother is not only alive but *vital,* a person that enjoys life and transmits the capacity to enjoy it to her offspring.

Through mimetic learning, her children take possession of this state of well-being. She is the *first joy-transmitter,* teaching life (in the broad sense of the word) to the *infans* from the point when they were in the womb. Thus, she reduces the traumatizing power of primal fantasies and of narcissistic and oedipal conflicts.

It is not easy to determine exactly what the structural role played by a joyful mother is, but we can safely say that she has a great influence in the potential consolidation of a core of basic trust in the child's psyche.

This kind of mother enjoys her motherhood. Her internalized joyful object gives her the needed inner confidence to face or minimize the difficulties of everyday life. She is diametrically opposite the figure of the 'dead mother' described by Green (1980, pp. 209–238).

The joyful mother causes:

1. the continuous facilitation of psychic well-being in the child and the parents;
2. the reduction of thanatic, masochistic potency;
3. the learning of healthy habits; and
4. the creation of a protective covering of happiness which surrounds both mother and child, and also mother and the family unit as a whole. This constitutes one of the many variants of the protective covering of positivity.

The joyful mother enables:

1. the child's identification with his or her vivifying attributes;
2. the incorporation of a good internal object that alleviates and lightens the psyche, since she is a 'trustable external object' (García Badaracco, 1985, p. 499);
3. the building of a healthy, non-conflict foundation for sexuality–sensuality; and
4. the formation of a benevolent superego, a guardian of life and well-being.

To be born as the child of a joyful mother is a beautiful beginning to a person's life. Undoubtedly, she will facilitate the child's psychical life, though she is not a sufficient condition to guarantee the *infans'* emotional stability. The processes of health and illness are not ruled by simple, deterministic cause–effect linearity. The multidetermined human interchanges and their psychical consequences require what Morin (1990) called 'complex thought' to be taken into account.

I would like to emphasize that on their way to adulthood, children are influenced by the proximity of *any joyful significant other*. To internalize joy, the child must introject an *internal joyful object* through multiple experiences with joy-transmitting significant others.

No psychical object can be the sole owner of the psychical fate of another. A happy father, happy siblings, a happy family constellation, and happy teachers: these are, among many others, vectors of positive influence in the education and development of a person. To focus excessively on specific aspects of the mother in order to understand her children's psychical development is to give her a quasi-omnipotent place in structuring their psyche. This notion is associated with the imaginary conception of a phallic mother. By appearing to make her the most important actor, there is a risk of blaming her disproportionately when, at some point in her life, her child 'fails'. At this juncture, all eyes fall upon her and the condemnation is devastating. The great engenderer becomes the great culprit of her child's every wrongdoing.

It is undeniable that the mother has the privilege of being a mediator between the *infans'* biology and their early extrauterine experiences. Due to her somatic union with the *infans* and the helplessness of the child, she has the power to inaugurate a dyad between both. The affect of joy (as happens with other affects) is *made flesh* in the child: between two people who have shared the same body there is *a shared psychical flesh.*

When a child has been joyfully mothered, their identification with the joyful traits of the adult's psyche provides them—if certain complex favourable circumstances are added—with the gifts of good humour, laughter, the enjoyment of jokes, and the ability to minimize unpleasant events. Life is valued according to the number of happy moments experienced. The ego ideal is built with ideally good representations closely related to the promotion of satisfactory experiences. The ideal goal of enjoying life at every moment prevails absolutely over narcissistic ideal ambitions such as to be rich, famous and powerful.

When happiness has primacy, the psyche is able to free itself of its neurosis.

b) The conquest of joy

This can be a conquest or a reconquest; in both cases, adverse circumstances have deprived the individual of the feeling of joy. If the absence of joy derives from an inner punishment in the face of an anti-ethical conscience, a process of reparation must take place to relieve the individual's bitterness.

Alienating identifications and the loss of one's authentic desire drain the psyche of its life-force and cause chronic sadness. Analytic treatment, which facilitates the process of dis-identification, plays a significant role in the reconquest of joy.

Joy may be lost over the course of time on account of a succession of unhappy experiences: pathological parental divorce, traumatic exile, sexual abuse, and so on. Under these circumstances, the good internal object is overwhelmed by conflicts and traumas. The joy of old is just a memory.

When masochistic pleasure prevents the process of working-through in mourning, and when narcissistic pathologies and the 'unconscious hatred of life'[3] prevail, the individual cannot recover their trust in good internal and external objects. As a consequence, they remain chronically bound to bitterness and despair.

To recover joy, not only will new, pleasant experiences able to neutralize suffering be needed, but also a great deal of inner, psychic work. Overcoming resentment, the patient's inner reconciliation with the aggressor, and the acceptance of their own fate, are all psychical processes that contribute to neutralizing hatred and, therefore, to releasing positive feelings.

c) Stolen joy

Individuals who are blocked from expressing joy persist in their sullen or indifferent attitude even on the happiest of occasions. The feeling of joy is suppressed.

There are situations which rob the individual of their happiness for a long time although they nevertheless fight to defend against that robbery. Whatever their age, when the external world deprives them of their joy, they look for a remedy in the form of well-being that temporarily alleviates their pathogenic suffering.

---

[3] Charles Bollas used this phrase during a lecture given at the Argentine Psychoanalytic Association.

While in the external world joy is destroyed by extreme traumatizing experiences, in the inner world it is annihilated by mental illness and the pain of living.

Overly destructive social processes such as dictatorships and genocides have robbed several generations of their joy and left them immersed in the collective tragedy of social horror.

To keep joy alive, in spite of all the grief and sorrows of life, three things are needed:

1) The building of a solid 'nucleus of stonerock core'
(Alizade, 1999, Chapter 2, pp. 25–34)
The 'rock core' is an inner space that constitutes a sort of psychic centre of gravity, providing a focal point of energy and strength. It constitutes a stabilizing force which may or may not be consolidated over the course of an individual's life. Like the roots of a tree, it sustains and stabilizes the subject, providing an inner strength. Driven by this force, the soma and psyche operate synergically. Although this space is generated in the interaction with the individual's environment, it requires a state of positive solitude where the person can retreat within him or herself, taking refuge within the fertile terrain of their intrasubjectivity.

2) The reconciliation with the hostile object (the 'enemy')
This involves overcoming resentment and the gradual decathexis of pathogenic and traumatic representation-affect complexes. It is based on the assumption that overcoming hateful feelings is a way to release the psyche so that the energy bound to hateful representations can become available again. In contrast, brooding over one's desire for revenge and destruction tends to backfire upon the suffering individual—as the death drive loops back upon itself—diminishing physical and mental well-being.

The energy released through decathecting the *complex of the enemy* allows the person to renew their 'mental circuitry' enabling them to improve their quality of life.

3) The fluidity of the libido
If the libido's viscosity is low, the process of working-through and the suppression of suffering are facilitated, enabling the pain of mourning and distress to be more easily overcome.

Psychical qualities that facilitate the attainment of joy

a) Psychical lightness

One of the main prerequisites for experiencing happiness is 'psychical lightness' (Freud's *Erleichterung*) (Freud, 1905c), to attain which unpleasant representations must be at least temporarily decathected. As was mentioned above, individuals that have suffered extreme traumas, such as those associated with historic or familial horror, may experience a temporary state of happiness thanks to the mechanism of psychical splitting. However, it is unlikely that they can become truly joyful people. The world of horror has deprived them of their potential for happiness as a result of the painful hyper-stimulation of mind and body, and the knowledge of the scope of sadism and perversity, which has been made flesh in them.

b) Mental calm (un-thinking)

This involves interrupting the constant activity of mental circuits which fixate on certain networks of conflictive representations and affects. The individual is able to stop dwelling on past conflicts and instead connects with the present. To acquire this ability, an inner process of working-through, which puts an end to the excess of representations flooding the psyche, is needed.

This mechanism could be called 'un-thinking'. To diminish or silence this *mental rumination* certain conditions must be fulfilled, such as mental discipline and the acquisition of mental automatisms. This incessant thinking wears the mind out and causes a lack of vitality and neurotic impoverishment owing to the blockage of free mental functioning.

Psychoanalytical treatment demands a certain amount of mental calm to facilitate the process of working-through. A consequence of this is that an excess of interpretations may hinder the progress of the treatment.

c) Capacity for object-relations and for object-loss

The joyful person is the one who has learnt to lose … and to recover. The structuring relationship of presence-absence, *'fort-da'*, (Freud, 1920g, pp. 14–15) results in the incorporation of a good reassuring internal object.

The suffering individual can withstand the painful process of mourning as they are sustained by their inner certainty in finding substitutes for what they have lost. Basic trust is a necessary condition to achieve joy.

d) Aesthetic sensitivity

The beauty of everyday things is a natural source of joy. Human beings derive pleasure from gratifying everyday contemplations.

Winnicott (1958, p. 34) liked to call these moments 'ego orgasms', meaning a climax in an ego experience bordering on ecstasy. These aesthetic, contemplative 'orgasms' are part of the process of sublimation.

Sensitivity to beauty generates happiness. It allows the individual to comprehend all those gratifying experiences—produced by a beautiful landscape, by the sound of the wind, by an inner light—that need only an aesthetic facilitation to be appreciated. The multiplicity of sensory experiences opens the door to a coenesthetic, sensorial universe in which the beautiful, the sublime and the insignificant coalesce.

e) Incorporating ethics through learning

Ethics are transmitted. There are familial and social ways to learn ethics—at school, in peer groups, in the workplace. Every generation teaches values and appropriate conduct to their youth. Everyday morality is the forerunner of ethical development.

The gradual acquisition of ethical values contributes to the individual's development on their way to maturity. The feeling of solidarity increases, producing ineffable sensations of well-being.

Maturity manifests itself in the concern for the 'far-away object' (Alizade, 1995, Chapter 5, p. 104) and in several expressions of 'tertiary narcissism' (ibid., pp. 98–107): acceptance of the finitude of one's life and of the transient character of the human condition, adoption of the principle of relativity, and the divestment of narcissism.

Erikson (1997, p. 111) said that there were seven cycles of human development; in the last one, under favourable conditions, 'generativeness' is achieved. He states that this 'generativeness' is composed of three elements: procreativity, productivity, and creativity, a triad from which there results a new virtue: care—caring about one's own ideas, products, and creations. This is transmitted from generation to generation and makes up the true wealth of humanity.

Actions born out of solidarity for other human beings and which are linked to beneficence are a source of inner joy.

Joy in different stages of life

1) The joy of innocence (of ignorance)

Children may learn to be happy in an environment of containment and fun. In the midst of their frustrations, tantrums, and difficulties, they always find a human being 'at hand' who is able to help. The necessary and positive limitations imposed on them contribute to their development.

The child incorporates a good object that is a source of joy: a 'joyful object'. Joy is the carrier of good health.

For the adult, the child's happiness is refreshing. The product of play and the spontaneous expression of emotions, it is the expression of innocence and the present in their purest form.

2) The hipomaniac joy of adolescence

'The world was mine,/I was the king.' The fantasmatic experience of completeness is resplendent in these poet's words.

The period of transition between childhood and youth is one which contains moments of euphoria. Affects are intense, whether they be linked to the enjoyment of life with one's peers or to the expression of rebellion, hatred, and depression. Happiness bursts onto the scene: it is the time of romance, adventure, and fun. Everything is new; everything that is good is young. It is also the time of triumph over parents and of excess—the negative counterpart being the taking of risks, potential accidents, the rejection of norms, and a dangerous sense of omnipotence.

3) The joy of maturity (of attachment and responsibility)

At this stage of the journey through life, the human being takes on responsibilities such as earning a living, managing the relationship with their partner, raising their children, caring for their parents, and so on.

Attachment, understood as the cathexis of objects both near (significant others) and far, brings the individual face to face with the issues of social leadership and the realization of social ideals.

The feeling of happiness largely depends on ethical achievements and of the inner preservation of the joyful object in the face of the inevitable harshness of life.

4) The joy of old age (of wisdom and detachment)
Old age implies longevity, a longevity that has a social impact. Longevity is devalued in the West, where old people are often shunned and marginalized, whereas it is highly valued in the East, where it is deemed to have an almost sacred character. Here it is not only wisdom which is attributed to the old (who may or may not have developed this attribute) but also experience. The old men have a place of honour at the table and their relatives endeavour to please them.

In old age, joy demands a certain level of psychophysical health but it is also the consequence of the elaborative work the individual has done with respect to their inner world through the different stages of life. In essence, this work involves the transformation of narcissism and the acceptance of the principle of relativity (Alizade, 1995, Chapter 5).

Old people need to be protected. If they are cared for and loved (as they have been in their childhood), they are able to enjoy their old age.

The process of detachment gives rise to a feeling of inner freedom. Old people say goodbye to their affects and objects in a gradual decathexis that soothes their mind. Though they would like to go on living, they accept that the stretch of life they have yet to cover is a short one, and serenely wait for the end.

Thankfulness

In the act of thanking, ethics and joy intertwine. To thank was for Heidegger 'the supreme act of human dignity and celebration' (quoted by Yafar, 1999, p. 22). Joy then acquires great importance, growing from the smallness of laughter to the heights of intimacy, the result of the satisfaction in one's own ability to acknowledge the goodness of a fellow human being. This acknowledgement increases the value both of the thanks-giver and of the thanked and a current of empathy flows between the two poles. In a sort of off-centering with regard to their own self, each individual pays tribute to the other, this being at the core of any gesture of sincere gratitude.

When one human being thanks another, they elevate themselves. Gratitude may be accompanied by reparation (Klein's *Wiedergutmachung*), insofar as primal feelings of hostility, envy and guilt are overcome to heal what has been damaged.

Gratitude ranges from the all-embracing 'thanks to life' to the small acts of gratitude that intersperse the succession of happy experiences in our everyday existence. The mere fact of having received the 'grace'* of life and the opportunity to experience its vicissitudes is reason enough to express gratitude—to God, to circumstance, to blissful chance—even when there is no specific object which one must thank.

Thankfulness is calming, since it reconciles the individual with their fate.

Joy and death

a) Knowledge and joy

There is nothing new in knowing that one is going to die. It is a knowledge both rational and universal. However, when this knowledge is rooted in one's own flesh and is actually experienced, there is a qualitative difference. For this to happen, there must be a threat of a serious illness or of a life-threatening situation whose signifier is connected with the semantics of annihilation. The fear and the anguish transmitted by this body-knowledge overwhelm the individual who is threatened in this way. Not even those people who have worked through their impermanence through experiences of detachment are safe when confronted by the shock of an impending death and of physical deterioration, with all its real and fantasized implications: pain, functional loss, disability, mutilation, and so on.

The certainty of finitude, when made flesh, marks the beginning of an unbearable time of psychical suffering both for the individual that is near to death and for those that surround them. It is almost inconceivable that a human being may experience pleasant feelings when faced with the loss of their own life.

This suffering is exacerbated by society's collective fantasy to flee from the knowledge of death, and the mandate of the superego to

---

*A play on words, since in Spanish the terms used to say 'the grace' and 'thanks' are very similar: *la gracia, (dar) las gracias*. (Translator's note.)

be healthy: a tacit, omnipresent ideal. The feeling that death is unfair increases when the person threatened with death is young, or has the responsibility of raising young children, or has projects that will remain unfinished. Thus, *not-knowing* the outcome is seen to be positive. The individual's defences attempt to deny the evidence, with its disruptive and disorganizing effect, and hope often takes on an absurd, deceptive guise. The individual is forced to confront despair.

But this knowledge may also trigger an intrapsychic, bonding process within the family which enables the elaboration of life in its totality and a fuller understanding of its true dimension. This process involves working-through 'universal trauma' in order to expand the individual's world view of reality so that this embraces the transient character of human life.

b) Dying joyfully

'I have always heard that one needs to die with joy,' said Socrates in Plato's *Phaedo*, and these words still sound to us incomprehensible if not bizarre. But in a second reading, perhaps we can grasp their transcendence, and the joy alluded to may be like a flash of light, a strange act of extreme enlightenment and bliss before the imminent great journey. It is a kind of secret, profound happiness that encompasses the gratitude of having had the opportunity to live. It is the joy of wisdom.

It cannot be denied that death is as painful as a change of skin. This pain may take the form of chronic, sterile suffering, or it may become—if it is worked through—a fertile terrain for a psychophysical transformation, allowing the individual to dare to experience the adventure of dying in the most lucid way. When I speak about the joy of dying, I mean a psychical attitude that focuses on the most intimate places of one's inner self. When human beings are mature enough to die, they live their death intensely even in their death throes, as they consciously perceive, to a greater or lesser extent, their body withdrawing from life. They experience the mutation of the organic, as an intact, complete body, into some organic disorganized substance, transforming them into a corpse in the quasi-miraculous process of their inevitable death. Paraphrasing Winnicott, we could say they are then in a transitional space leading to death, in a state of repose, where they surrender to the ludic, unknown states prior to death (Alizade, 1995).

Here the manifest (pure suffering, the painful process of extinction) and the latent (that which is invisible for those who observe the dying person) are most frequently dissociated. The previously felt happiness is absorbed into an intimate space within the self, in an almost incomprehensible acceptance of fate.

Joyful death is not at all encouraged in our culture, where the idea of forbidden death (Aries, 1974) prevails instead. The consumer society, competitiveness, and the exaggerated cult of youth, health and the body beautiful lead people to deny the reality of death being possible at any moment.

Joyful death is an erotic, peaceful kind of death. Feeling joyful in the face of death requires the following:

a. the attainment of psychical maturity;
b. thankfulness for having had the opportunity to live;
c. the acceptance of fate;
d. the divestment of narcissism and the exploration of psychical spaces beyond the ego;
e. the relativization of failure;
f. the expansion of the *Weltanschaung*; and
g. the attainment to some degree of integrity and wisdom.

For individuals who are prepared to die happily, the experience and representation of being part of an infinite whole is a familiar one. They become one with the universe mimetically and fantasmatically.

The marvel of creation, introjected through the sensual-affective contemplation of nature and culture, becomes an inexhaustible source of pleasure for them. With this heightened aesthetic sense, from the smallness of one's own insignificance, the beautiful and the creative are resplendent. The introjection of multiple sensibilities opens the mind to a new, receptive, positive dimension.

Beauty flows forth, and the inexorable order proclaims the end and the transformation of everything. Facing the ultimate boundary, happiness emerges. The submission and servitude to the superior order of nature soothes and eases the individual's passage to death. The attachment to the material and the affective slowly fades.

The mysterious, magic experience of the unknown ahead expands the individual's fantasmatic potential: everything is possible, and death becomes a strange opportunity to bring about an unimaginable, transcendent experience. Reality is no longer dominated by suffering. Once this has been defeated, reality takes on a grand, transcendent quality.

Joy is then transmuted into an adventure, a desire to know more. The body loses its strength and departs ... and before the dying person's eyes, the whole universe opens up.

CLOSING WORDS

Each life is uniquely crafted and requires creativity to shape the most beautiful forms possible.

The art of living is an ideal which we strive for. To realize this ideal, we try in our everyday life to cultivate our potential to achieve a state of well-being. Unfortunately, psychic death and neurosis lie in wait and all too often rob us of the best of our lives.

I have no doubt that the business of living, as Pavese calls it, is difficult.

Time and again, the expression of the life instinct encounters obstacles. The struggle for good health and 'the defence of happiness', as in Joan Manuel Serrat's song, are of prime importance, even more so in today's societies whose governments fail to give priority to the care, protection and happiness of their citizens.

The art of living goes hand in hand with the art of dying. Earthly pleasures are more fully appreciated when the ephemerality of our existence has a silent presence in our consciousness.

The art of healing is highlighted in this text, which now comes to a close.

The aim of this book is to contribute to the creation of well-being in our patients and to the improvement of their mental health, and also to the development of analytical treatment which embraces the expression of happiness in its multiplicity of forms.

REFERENCES

Abbagnano, N. (1996). *Diccionario de Filosofía*. México: Fondo de Cultura Económica.

Alizade, A.M. (1982). *The inner setting*. Unpublished.

Alizade, A.M. (1992 [1999]). *La sensualidad femenina*. Buenos Aires: Amorrortu editores. English edition. *Feminine Sensuality*. London: Karnac.

Alizade, A.M. (1992). Nada de Mujer. In: *La Sensualidad Femenina*. Buenos Aires: Amorrotu editores. pp. 209–217.

Alizade, A.M., Aptekman, M., Gerst, W., Siedmann de Armesto, M., Weissmann, F. & Weissmann, J.C. (1993). El psicoanalista enfrenta el horror. *Rev. de Psicoan, L*: 4/5. pp. 767–780.

Alizade, A.M. (1995). *Clínica con la muerte*. (Near death. Clinical studies.) Buenos Aires: Amorrortu editores.

Alizade, A.M. (1996b). Mesa redonda. Pensando la clínica y la psicopatología actuales. In: *Rev. Asociación Escuela Argentina de Psicoterapia para Graduados*, N. 22, pag 43 y descriptor de este concepto en la Comisión de Informática de dicha Escuela, julio 1997.

Alizade, A.M. (1996c). La sexualidad y los condicionamientos culturales. In: *Freud y su tiempo. Depto* de Historia de la Asoc. Psicoanalítica Argentina, pp. 101–107.

Alizade, A.M. (1999b). El sustrato sensual-afectivo y la estructuración psíquica (Sensualidad y afectos). Trabajo presentado en el Congreso de Santiago de Chile en el marco de la IPA, julio 1999. *Rev. de psicoan. T LVI, 3*: 579–590.

Alizade, A.M. (1999c). El encuadre interno. (The inner setting.) *revista Zona erógena* No 41. Buenos Aires: Las Neurosis en la actualidad, 1999.

Alizade, A.M. (2000). Duelos del cuerpo. In: A.M. Alizade (Ed.), *Asociación Psicoanalítica del Uruguay*. Mayo: Montevideo, 2000.

Alizade, A.M. (2002). The fluidity of the female universe and its psychic consequences. In: A.M. Alizade (Ed.) *The Embodied Female*. London: Karnac. Psyxchoanalysis and Women Series, pp. 25–36.

Anzieu, D. (1970). *Elements d'une théorie de l'interprétation*. Paris: Puf.

Anzieu, D. (1985 [1989]). *The skin ego* (Chris Turner, Trans.). New Haven, CT: Yale University Press.

Anzieu, D. (1990). *Une peau pour les pensées*. Paris: Editions Apsygée.

Anzieu, D. (1990b). *L'épiderme nomade et la peau psychique*. Paris: Editions Apsygée.

Aries, P. (1974). *Western Attitudes Toward Death: From the Middle Ages to the Present*. USA: Johns Hopkins University Press.

Aslan, C.M. (1993). La repetición que depende de las estructuras. *Rev. de Psicoanálisis, Número especial internacional, 1993*, 2: 11–19.

Baranger, M. & W. (1961–1962). La situación analítica como campo dinámico. In: *Problemas del campo psicoanalítico*. Buenos Aires, 1993. pp. 129–164.

Baranger, M. & W. (1964). El insight' en la situación analítica. In: *Problemas del Campo Analítico*. Kargieman: Buenos Aires, 1993. pp. 165–177.

Baranger, M., Baranger, W. & Mom, J.M. (1988). The Infantile Psychic Trauma from Us to Freud: Pure Trauma, Retroactivity and Reconstruction. *Int. J. Psycho-Anal., 69*: 113–128.

Breuer, J. & Freud, S. (1895d [1893–1895]). Studies on Hysteria. Chapter IV *The Psychotherapy of Hysteria, SE, Vol II*.

Blanton, S. (1930 [1971]). *Diary of my analysis with Sigmund Freud*. New York: Hawthorn Books, Inc.

Bleger, J. (1967). *Psicoanálisis del encuadre psicoanalítico. cap.VI de Simbiosis y Ambiguedad*. Buenos Aires: editorial Paidós.

Blos, P. (1979). *The Adolescent Passage. Developmental Issues*. New York: International Universities, Inc.

Bowlby, J. (1989). *Una base segura. Aplicaciones clínicas de una teoría del apego*. Buenos Aires: Paidós.

Cardozo de Suárez, E., Rusconi, R. & Bondorevsky, M. (1983). La realidad en Freud, lo Real en Lacan. *Rev. de Psicoan.T.XL, 5/6*: 1123–1140.

Dolto, F. (1982). *La sexualite fémenine*. (Feminine Sexuality). Paris, Scarabée et compagnie. Le livre de Poche.

Eliot, T.S. (1930). *Four cuartets*. Burnt Norton.

Erikson, E. (1997). *The Life Cycle Completed*. New York–London: W-W Norton and Company.

Etchegoyen, H. (1986). 'Impasse' and the basic principles of psychoanalytic technique. In: *Fundamentals of Psychoanalytic Technique*. New York: Brunner/Mazel, 1991.

Etchegoyen. H. (1999). *Un ensayo sobre la interpretación psicoanalitica*. Buenos Aires: Editorial Polemos, Chapter 1.

Faladé, S. (1980). Sobre lo real. (On the real.) In: *Actas de la Escuela Freudiana de París* (pp. 37–44). VII Congreso, Roma 1974. Spain: ediciones Petrel, 1980.

Ferenczi, S. (1913). Stages in the development of the sense of reality. In: *Sex in Psychoanalysis*. New York: Dover, 1956.

Ferrater, M. (1941 [1965]). *Diccionario de filosofía*. Buenos Aires: editorial Sudamericana.

Fliess, R. (1949). Silencio y verbalización. Suplemento a la teoría de la regla analítica. In: Nasio, J.D. (comp.) *El silencio en psicoanálisis*. Buenos Aires: ediciones Amorrortu, 1988. pp. 57–75.

Freud, S. & Breuer, J. (1893a). On the psychical mechanism of hysterical phenomena: preliminary communication. *SE, Vol II*.

Freud, S. (1900a). The interpretation of dreams. *SE, Vol IV*.

Freud, S. (1905a [1904]). On psychotherapy. *SE, Vol VII*.

Freud, S. (1905c). Jokes and their relations to the Unconscious. *SE, Vol 8*.

Freud, S. (1905e [1901]). Fragment of an Análysis of a Case of Hysteria. *SE Vol 7*.

Freud, S. (1912–1913). Totem and Taboo. *SE, Vol 13*.

Freud, S. (1913c). On beginning the treatment. *SE, Vol 12*.

Freud, S. (1913i). The Disposition to Obsessional Neurosis. *SE, Vol XII*.

Freud, S. (1914c). On Narcissism: an Introduction. *SE, Vol 14I*.

Freud, S. (1914g). Remembering, Repeating and Working-Through. *SE, Vol 12*.

Freud, S. (1915c). Instincts and their vicissitudes. *SE Vol XIV*, p. 136.

Freud, S. (1915e). The Unconscious, Unconscious Emotions. *SE, Vol 14*, Chap. 3.

Freud, S. (1915f). A Case of Paranoia running Counter to the Psycho-Analytic Theory of the Disease. *SE, Vol 14*, p. 269.

Freud, S. (1917e [1915]). Mourning and Melancolía. *SE, Vol 14*.

Freud, S. (1916–1917). Introductory Lectures on Psycho-Analysis. *SE, Vol 16*.

Freud, S (1919d). Introduction to psychoanalysis and the war neurosis. *SE, Vol XVII*.

Freud, S. (1919h). The 'uncanny'. *SE, Vol XVII*.

Freud, S. (1920g). Beyond the Pleasure Principle. *SE, Vol 18*.

Freud, S. (1923b). The ego and the id. *SE, Vol 19*.

Freud, S. (1925h). Negation. *SE, Vol 19*.

Freud, S. (1933a [1932]). Dissection of the Personality, Lecture No XXXI, New Introductory Lectures on Psycho-analysis. *SE, Vol XXII*.

Freud, S. (1937c). Analysis Terminable and Interminable. *SE, Vol XXIII*.

Freud, S. (1940a [1938]). An outline of psychoanalysis. *SE, Vol XXIII*.

Freud, S. (1950a [1887–1902]). Project for a Scientific Psychology. *SE, Vol 1*.

Fullat, O. & Gomis, C. (1984). *El hombre, un animal ético*. Barcelona: editorial vicens-vives, Biblioteca didáctica de filosofía.

García Badaracco, J. (1985). Identification and its Vicissitudes in the Psychoses. The Importance of the Concept of the 'Maddening Object'. *Int J Psycho-Anal., 67*: 133–146.

Garma, A., Allegro L., Z. de Arbiser S., Arbiser A., L. de Ferrer S., Garma, E., Salas, E., Schlossberg, T., Weissman, F. & Winocur, J. (1978). La realidad y la fantasía del hombre contemporáneo. (Reality and fantasy of contemporary man.) *Rev. de Psicoan. T XXXV, 5*: 1035–1042.

Garma, A. & Garma, E. (1973). Reacciones maníacas: alegría masoquista del yo por el triunfo, mediante engaños, del superyó. In: *La fascinación de la muerte*. Buenos Aires: editorial Paidós.

Green, A. (1980). The dead mother. In: *Life Narcissism, Death Narcissism*. Free Associations Books, 2001.

Green, A. (1993). *The Work of the Negative* (translated by Andrew Weller). Free Association Books, 1999.

Greenson, R. & Wexler, M. (1969). The non-transference relationship in the psychoanalytic situation. *Int. J. Psycho-Anal. 50*: 27–39.

Grotjhan, M. (1957). *Beyond Laughter*. New York: Mc Graw-Hill Book Company, Inc.

Gubrich-Simitis, I. (1979). Extreme traumatization as cumulative trauma. In: *The Psychoanalytic Study of the Child, 36*: 415–450.

Hartmann, H. (1958). The conflict-free Ego Sphere. In: *Ego Psychology and the Problem of Adaptation* (pp. 3–21). New York: Int. University Press.

Heiddeger, D. (2004). *Heidegger y sus relaciones con el psicoanálisis*. Agenda 28. Viva: editorial Letra, p. 32.

Lacan, J. (1964). Présence de l'analyste. In: *Les quatre concepts fondamentaux de la psychoanalyse*. Cap X: 113–122.

Lacan, J. (1973 [1998]). The presence of the analyst. In: *The four fundamental concepts of Psychoanalysis*. New York: W.W, Norton and Company.

Laplanche, P. (1968 [1971]). *Diccionario de Psicoanálisis*. Barcelona: Labor.

Lorand, S. (1946). *Technique of Psychoanalytic Therapy*, New York: Int. University Press, 1948.

Maldonado, J. (1975). Impasse y 'mala fe' en el análisis de un paciente. *Rev. de Psicoanálisis, T XXXII, 1.*

Marucco, N. (1996). Recordar, repetir, elaborar. In: *Cura analítica y transferencia*. Buenos Aires: Amorrortu editores, 1998, pp. 252–268.

Marucco, N. (1996). Recordar, repetir, elaborar. In: Zona erógena, 1996, n 30, pag. 41. Cap. 16 de Cura analítica y transferencia. Buenos Aires: Amorrortu editores, 1998.

Monedero, C. (1970). *La Alegría. Un análisis fenomenológico y antropológico*. Madrid: Mateu-Cromo Artes Gráficas.

Morin, E. (1990). *Introduction à la pensée complexe*. Paris: ESF éditeur.

Nacht, S. (1962). The curative factors in psycho-analysis. *International Journal of Psychoanalysis, 43*: 206–11.

Nasio, J.D. (1980). *L'Inconscient à venir*. Paris: Christian Bourgois, éditeur.

Perren-Klinger, G. (1996). Human reactions to traumatic experience: from patogenetic to salutogenetic thinking. In: *Trauma: From Individual Helplessness to group resources*. Berne, Switzerland: Paul Haupt Publishers. (Footnote 29, p. 18.)

Pichon-Rivière, E. (1970). *Clases dictadas en la primera escuela privada de Psicología Social.*

Pichon-Rivière, E. (1970). *El proceso grupal. Del Psicoanalisis a la Psicologia social.* Buenes Aires: Nueva Visión.

Platon. *Fedón o sobre el alma*. S.A. España: Editorial Bruguera. 1975. pp. 137–149.

Popper, K. (1934). The scientific method. In: D. Miller (Ed.), *Popper Selections*. USA: Princeton Univ. Press, 1985.

Popper, K. (1945). The defence of Rationalism. In: D. Miller (Ed.), *Popper Selections*. USA: Princeton Univ. Press, 1985.

Popper, K. (1958). The origins of rationalism. In: D. Miller (Ed.), *Popper Selections*. USA: Princeton Univ. Press, 1985.

Popper, K. (1992). La televisión corrompe a la humanidad. Es como la guerra. In: *La Lección de este Siglo* (pp. 93–97). (Lesson of this Century: With Two Talks on Freedom and the Democratic State. Interviewed by Giancarlo Bosetti. Translated by Patrick Camiller.) Buenos Aires: Temas grupo editorial, 1998.

Pragier, (1990). Un siècle après l'Esquissse: Nouvelles métaphores, métaphores du nouveau. *Rev. Francaise de Psychoanalyse, LIV* : 6.

Puget, J., de Bianchedi, E.T., Bianchedi, M., Braun, J. & Pelento, M. (1993). Status psicoanalítico de la violencia social. In: *Revista de Psicoanálisis, L*: 4/5. pp. 991–998.

Racker, H. (1959). Sobre técnica clásica y técnicas actuales del psicoanálisis estudio II. In: *Estudios sobre Técnica Psicoanalítica*. México: Paidós, 1990.

Reik, T. (1926). En el principio es el silencio. In J.D. Nasio (Ed.), *El silencio en psicoanálisis*. Buenos Aires, Amorrortu Editores. 1987, pp. 21-26.

Rimbaud, A. (1873). *Une Saison en enfer*. Paris: Mercure de France, 1952.

Rosenberg, B. (1991). *Masochisme mortifère et masochisme gardien de la vie*. Paris: PUF.

Rosolato, G. (1989). Lo negativo y su léxico. In: *Lo Negativo* (pp. 23–38). Buenos Aires: Amorrortu editores, 1991.

Roudinesco, E. y Plon, M. (1997). *Diccionario de Psicoanálisis*. Buenos Aires: Paidós.

Sahovaler, J. (1997). *Psicoanálisis de la televisión*. Buenos Aires: ediciones el Otro.

Sófocles (1985). Edipo en Colono. In: *Tragedias*. España: EDAF.

Spinoza, B. (1987). Ética. Madrid. Alianza Editorial.

Spitz, R. (1965). *First year of Life: Psychoanalytic Study of normal and deviant object relations*. New York: International Universities Press, Inc.

Thom, R. (1980). *Parábolas y catástrofes*. España, Tusquets editores, Superínfimos 5, 1985.

Valls, J. (2004). Cantidad, memoria y deseo. In: *Metapsicología y Modernidad. El Proyecto freudiano*. Buenos Aires: Lugar Editorial, pp. 59–66.

Winnicott, D. (1941). The observation of infants in a set situation. *Int. Jo. 22: 229–249.*

Winnicott, D. (1958). Capacity to be alone. In: *The Madurational Processes and the Facilitating Environment*. London: The Hogarth Press and the Institute of Psychoanalysis, 1965, pp. 29–36.

Yafar, R. (1999). *Algunas reflexiones sobre el pensamiento poetizador en la obra de Martin Heidegger y sus relaciones con el psicoanálisis*. Dossier Heiddeger, Agenda 28, Buenos Aires, Letra Viva, 2004, p. 32.

INDEX

For Product Safety Concerns and Information please contact our EU
representative GPSR@taylorandfrancis.com
Taylor & Francis Verlag GmbH, Kaufingerstraße 24, 80331 München, Germany

www.ingramcontent.com/pod-product-compliance
Ingram Content Group UK Ltd.
Pitfield, Milton Keynes, MK11 3LW, UK
UKHW022025061126
477531UK00002B/35

* 9 7 8 0 3 6 7 3 2 6 2 1 0 *